The Three Addit.

A Study

William Heaford Daubney

Alpha Editions

This edition published in 2023

ISBN : 9789357944854

Design and Setting By
Alpha Editions
www.alphaedis.com
Email - info@alphaedis.com

PREFACE

The three apocryphal portions of Daniel considered in this book have often been hardly judged. One of them had almost become a byword of contempt for fabulous inventiveness. Yet the writer hopes that he has succeeded in shewing that they are worthy of more serious attention than they have frequently received. The prejudice long existing in this country against the Apocrypha as a whole has told heavily against two at any rate of these booklets; and he who attempts to investigate the nature and origin of the Additions to Daniel finds himself following a track which is anything but well beaten. The number of commentaries or treatises in English dealing directly with these works is very small. Indeed, considering the position accorded to them by the Church, it is surprisingly so. And of those which exist, some are not very valuable for accurate study. Hence, in preparing a treatise of this kind, materials have to be quarried and brought together from varied and distant sources; and the work, small as its result may be in size, has proved a laborious one. The conclusions arrived at on many points are but provisional; for the writer thinks that the day has not yet come when the source and place of these Additions to Daniel can be surely and incontrovertibly fixed. It is to be hoped that further evidence and longer study will eventually make these matters clearer than they are at present. Meanwhile, careful and unprejudiced work upon the subject, by whomsoever undertaken, cannot but tend towards that goal; and the author trusts that he may have contributed something which will help, at least a little, towards the solution of the difficult problem presented.

The Song of the Three and the Histories of Susanna and of Bel and the Dragon are most interesting memorials of the spirit of their time, though that time may be difficult to fix precisely. And when looked at from the religious point of view they are replete with valuable moral lessons for "example of life and instruction of manners," to borrow the terms which the Sixth Article of Religion employs with regard to the Apocryphal books. An attempt has been made, in a concluding chapter on each book, to draw some of these lessons out, so that they may be easily available for such homiletic and other purposes as are contemplated in that Article.

The study of these three pieces supplementary to Daniel has convinced the writer that they are of more value than has been generally supposed, and are worthy of the attention of biblical scholars in a much higher degree than that which has usually been accorded to them. If he has in any way helped in providing materials, or in suggesting ideas, which may fructify in abler hands, he will be rewarded for the researches he has made.

It appears to him that there is much connected with these books which we are unable now fully to discover; much about which it is unwise to dogmatize; many questions which must be treated as open ones; many problems which can at most only receive provisional solutions, till further facts are elicited and further insight given. The time is apparently still distant when the origin and true standing of these Additions can be certainly assigned to them: for, at the present, agreement amongst Christians on these points shews but little sign of being arrived at. Yet we trust that the time will come when deeper knowledge will make it possible for disputed points to be settled. "The patience of the godly shall not be frustrate" (Ecclus. xvi. 13).

In conclusion I must record my hearty thanks to Dr. Sinker, Librarian of Trinity College, Cambridge, for the great assistance he has given me in correcting the proof-sheets, as well as for his constant kindness in many other ways, of which these words are but an insufficient acknowledgment.

W.H.D.

ST. MARGARET'S GATE,
BURY ST. EDMUNDS.
St. Matthias' Day, 1906.

PART I
INTRODUCTION

INTRODUCTION.

These Additions differ from the other Apocryphal books, except the "rest of" Esther, in not claiming to be separate works, but appearing as supplements to a canonical book. The Song of the Three Children takes its assumed place between vv. 23 and 24 of Dan. iii.; the History of Susanna in the language of the A.V. is "set apart from the beginning of Daniel"; and Bel and the Dragon is "cut off from the end of" the same book. The first of these additions alone has an organic connection with the main narrative; the other two are independent scenes from the life, or what purports to be the life, of Daniel—episodes, one in his earlier, one in his later, career. In the Song, Daniel personally does not appear at all; in Susanna and in Bel he plays a conspicuous part; in Susanna appearing as a sort of 'deus ex machina' to set things right at the end; and in Bel he is an essential actor in the whole story.

It is hoped to shew, amongst other things, that the dissimilarity supposed to exist between these additions and the rest of Daniel is by no means so great as has sometimes been imagined. The opinion of one of the latest commentators on Daniel (Marti, Tübingen, 1901, p. xx) may be taken as a fair sample of this view. He thinks these pieces by no means congruous with the canonical Daniel: "Den Abstand dieser apokryphischen Erzählungen von dem in hebraram. Dan. aufgenommen Volkstradition kann niemand verkennen." So far as these additions to the contents of Daniel are concerned, he would agree with the exaggerated statement of Trommius as to all the Apocrypha: "ad libros canonicos S. Scripturæ proprie non pertinent nec cum Græca eorum versione quicquam commune habent," etc. (*Concord. Præf.* § xi.). The sharp distinction drawn by J.M. Fuller also between the style and thought of these additions, and of the canonical Daniel, is far too strong: "as clearly marked as between the canonical and apocryphal gospels." Few will think the separation between them so wide as this (*Speaker's Comm. Introd. to Dan.* p. 221a). Moreover, they are much less obviously incongruous, less plainly meant for edifying "improvements" by a later hand, than the Additions to Esther.

But beyond the connection, more or less strong, which these pieces have with the canonical book, they have also a connection, by means of certain similar features, with one another. All have this in common, viz. the celebration or record of some deliverance. God's persecuted people are rescued from mortal danger. In the first and third cases they suffer at the hands of idolaters; in the second, of Jewish co-religionists. In each case they provide us with a scene from Israelitish life "in a strange land." They are tales of the Babylonian Captivity.

In each story the ministry of angels, giving aid against visible foes, takes a prominent place; though in Susanna these appearances are suppressed in Theodotion's version, an angel, however, being just mentioned in Daniel's sentences of condemnation. In each case too there is distinct progress under God's guiding hand; things are left much better at the end than at the beginning. There is a tone of confidence, bred of sure conviction, in one abundantly expressed, in the others latent, as to the ultimate triumph of right. They agree in the certainty of God's defence, and shew complete reliance on Him. The Captivity had done a purifying work.

These stories of rescue from oppressors would be specially acceptable to the Jews of the Babylonian Captivity; more so probably than to the Jews of the Dispersion elsewhere. Howbeit they are records of zeal and trust which have moved many hearts in all ages and places.

In the last two Daniel appears as a person of great knowledge and power, successfully acting under the Divine guidance. In all three there is little which can properly be called strained or far-fetched. Almost everything is drawn naturally from what we may presume would be the condition of Daniel's time. Both behind and through the details of the stories we can see the heart of one who praised God, loved justice, and hated idolatry; who took delight in what was noble, pure, and truthful, and waged a successful warfare with whatever he encountered of an opposite character.

Each piece, moreover, has what may be thought to be its own allusion or reminiscence in the New Testament. And each of these parallels, curiously enough, seems eminently characteristic of the addition whence it may have been taken.

Thus we find in the parallel of St. Matt, xxvii. 24 with Susanna 46 the assertion of innocency in respect of miscarriage of justice; in that of Heb. xii. 23 with the Song 64 (86), the utterance of the spirits and souls of the righteous; and in that of Acts xvii. 23 with Bel and Dragon 27, the mocker of idols.

One is from the beginning, one from the midst, one from the end of the Greek Daniel; the first by St. Matthew reporting Pilate; the second by a writer not certainly identified; the third by St. Luke reporting St. Paul. These may be merely accidental resemblances, but their occurrence in this way is curious, and worthy of consideration.

As to the position of these pieces, whether in or out of the canon, it is probable, speaking generally, that those who used the Hebrew Bible, or versions uninfluenced by the LXX, disregarded them as not being part of Holy Scripture; and that those who used the LXX, or its versions, accepted them, either with or without hesitation. Under the chapters entitled "Early

Christian Literature" it will be seen that those were by no means wanting who appear to attribute in practical use canonical authority to each fragment; and at least what Otto Stähelin says of Clement of Alexandria, that he "nicht geringer schätzte," may be held true of nearly all the Fathers who name them (*Clem. Alex, und LXX*, Nürnberg, 1901, p. 74). It is, however, surprising that this divergence of use, in so important a matter as the extent of the canon, did not give rise to a more general controversy. What discussion there was on this question lay chiefly between a few scholarly individuals, who treated the matter as of private and personal, almost as much as of public, interest.

Even if it were admitted that these works were not in the Hebrew canon, the question is still not absolutely settled. For it might be contended, without at all asserting that the Hebrew canon was erroneous or deficient in its time, that these and other apocryphal works were reserved in the providence of God for the Christian Church to deal with as she thought fit. Nor is it clear that her powers as to them, when deciding for canonicity or no, were of necessity more restricted than her powers as to the N.T. books on the same question. What Tertullian says with regard to 'Enoch' might be extended to other books, "Scio scripturam Enoch... non recipi a quibusdam quia nec in armarium Judaicum admittitur... a vobis quidem nihil omnino rejiciendum est quod pertinent ad nos" (*De cult. fæm.* I. 13).

The title 'Daniel,' it should be observed, in lists of Scripture books, often covers these additions; as for example in Origen's list, as preserved by Eusebius, *H.E.* vi. 25. For we know that Origen (*Ep. ad Afric.*) defended these additions, and so almost certainly intended this title to include them. So also with Athanasius and Cyril of Jerusalem'(*see* Sus. 'Canonicity,' p. 160). Probably it is on this account that Loisy (*O.T. Canon*, Paris, 1890, p. 97) says that Athanasius received "certainement les fragments de Daniel, sur la foi des Septante, comme le font Origène et tous les Pères grecs."

Ecclesiastical practice, as well as their distribution amongst the canonical books of both Greek and Latin Bibles, told, as time went on, more and more in favour of their inclusion.

But they were not officially recognized as on a level in all respects with Holy Scripture, even by the Roman Church, till the fourth session of the Council of Trent (1546), when they were all placed on an equality with, in fact treated as portions of, the book of Daniel. Probably the phrase "libros integros *cum omnibus suis partibus*" was introduced into the decree with special reference to these additions and those to Esther. This decree, making them "sacred and canonical," was carried, according to Loisy (p. 201), by 44 placets to 3 non-placets and 5 doubtful.[1] Dr. Streane, however, says (*Age of the Maccabees*, 1898, p. 102) it was passed by "a small majority." Even writers so late as Nicholas de Lyra (†1340) and Denys the Carthusian (†1471) speak of these additions as true, but not parts of Holy Scripture (Loisy, p. 223, quoting Corn. à Lap. on Dan. xiii. 3). And they were of the Roman obedience.

[1] He refers to Theiner, *Acta ... concil. Trident,* i. 77.

Bleek (*Introd. to O.T.* II. 336, Eng. tr.) says that the seventh decree of the Council of Florence (1439), making mention of apocryphal books as canonical, which no one was acquainted with before the Tridentine Council, is very probably not genuine. Denys the Carthusian, it will be observed, was subsequent to the supposed Florentine decree, and seemingly ignorant of its existence.

The same writer states (pp. 336, 339) that while Karlstadt classed some of the Apocrypha as "hagiographa extra canonem," he called these supplements to Daniel, with the Prayer of Manasses, and others as "plane apocryphos." He also represents Luther as prettily styling these pieces corn-flowers plucked up, because not in the Hebrew, yet placed in a separate garden or bed, because much that is good is found in them. They are thus detached in his version, as in ours, from Daniel, and placed among the apocryphal books. Calvin, however, in his Lectures on Daniel entirely ignores these additions. His English translator barely mentions them in his preface (Edinb. 1852, p. xlix.).

Far more contemptuous than Luther's estimate of these productions is that of Professor (now Bishop) Ryle in the *Cambridge Companion to the Bible* (1894), where he writes: "The character of these stories is trifling and childish."

But in reply to this and similar depreciatory opinions, it may be pointed out that one does not look in these extra-Danielic stories for such a knowledge of the human heart as is displayed in the Psalms, nor for such knowledge of the Godhead as is revealed in St. John's Gospel. If we look for fully developed doctrine of this kind, we shall no doubt be disappointed. But we do find religious teaching after the tenor of the old covenant, such as might be expected in compositions which are mainly narrative; we meet with teaching which looks quite as clear as that, say, of the books of Ruth, Chronicles, or Esther. Indeed, those who have a mind to draw moral and spiritual instruction from these brief works will not find it difficult to do so, or discover that the religious teaching is out of harmony with that which is acknowledged to exist in Daniel (*see* chaps, on "Example of Life and Instruction of Manners"). In point of fact, an overgrowth of unreasonable objections has been too much encouraged; and if these pieces may not in all respects secure a favourable vote, it is desirable that they may receive at least an unprejudiced and equitable judgment.

The examples of patristic use given under the head of "Early Christian Literature" will, it is hoped, sufficiently refute such statements as that of

Albert Barnes (*Daniel*, Lond. 1853, pp. 79, 80): "It is seldom that these additions to Daniel are quoted or alluded to at all by the early Christian writers, but when they are, it is only that they may be condemned." This may be taken as a specimen of a certain class of adverse opinion, evidently formed without sufficient investigation of the subject. In reality, these pieces are referred to, considering their brevity, with surprising frequency; that the references are not exclusively, or even generally, for purposes of condemnation, hardly needs to be stated.

What effect these writings took on Jewish readers there is little or nothing to shew. With the rest of the LXX, they seem to have lost ground with Jews as they gained it with Christians. The closing scene of Bel and the Dragon, however, is made use of in *Breshith Rabba* to illustrate Joseph's abandonment in the pit (Gen. xxxvii.)[2]. To Christians indeed they have, from a very early date, constantly presented themselves as highly valuable for purposes of edification. Nor, with the possible exception of Susanna, is it easy to see in what way they could have furthered, in that aspect, any undesirable end.

[2] So Raymund Martini, at the end of his *Pugio fidei*; but his quotation has been doubted. *See* B. and D. 'Chronology,' p. 229.

What will be the future of these pieces by which, in the Greek Bible, the contents of Daniel were increased? It is not easy to say. Much will surely depend on the eventual consensus of opinion as to the date of that book itself. Neither the Roman nor Greek Churches shew any sign of modifying their entire,[3] or very slightly qualified, acceptance of these additions as integral parts of Holy Scripture. On the other hand, English-speaking Protestant Dissenters shew almost as little sign of rising to any religious appreciation of them.

[3] The Vatican Council confirmed the Tridentine decree on Scripture (*Const.* "Dei Filius" II., Loisy, p. 239).

Between these extremes the Church of England, and perhaps the German and Scandinavian Lutherans, hold, as to these books, an intermediate position, which in this, as in some other questions, may not improbably prove to be the right one. In any case the English Church has always treated them with great respect, a large part of one of them entering into her Morning Prayer, and the other two having been appointed as first lessons in her calendar from 1549 to 1872, except that Bel and the Dragon was removed from 1604 to 1662. Previous to this last date they were read, not as independent books, but as Dan. xiii. and xiv.

A patient waiting for the production of further evidence as to the origin and position of these additions can hardly be unrewarded. Meanwhile we may fitly agree with St. Gregory of Nazianzus' lines, which apply as well to these as to the other books of the Apocrypha:

Οὐκ ἅπασα βίβλος ἀσφαλὴς,
ἡ σεμνὸν ὄνομα τῆς Τραφῆς κεκτημένη.
εἰσὶν γὰρ, εἰσὶν ἔσθ᾽ ὅτε ψευδώνυμοι
βίβλοι· τινὲς μὲν ἔμμεσοι, καὶ γείτονες,
ὡς ἄν τις εἴποι, τῶν ἀληθείας λόγων.

(Poems, lib. II., ad Seleucum, 252-256; Migne, Patr. Gr. xxxvii. 1593.)

PART II
THE SONG OF THE THREE HOLY CHILDREN

בָּאֻרִים כַּבְּדוּ יְהֹוָ֖ה
(יש׳ כד׳ טו׳)

THE SONG OF THE THREE HOLY CHILDREN

ANALYSIS.

vv.

1, 2. Narrative in continuation of the canonical text, describing the procedure of the three children in the furnace.

3-22. Azarias' confession (3-10), and prayer (11-22), on behalf of them all.

23-28. Narrative describing the fire, the descent of the Angel, and the happy result.

29-68. The Song of praise itself, which may be subdivided thus: God directly addressed in blessing (29-34); after all God's works, celestial objects are addressed, including Angels[4] (35-41); objects of the lower heaven or atmosphere are called upon, including those immediately concerned, wind and dew being placed next to fire and heat (42-51); then the earth[5] and its natural features, and the animals inhabiting it, are called upon (52-59); then the human race, as a whole and in various classes, down to the three children themselves (60-66). In conclusion God is extolled for His ever-enduring mercy in phrases culled from the Psalter (67, 68).

[4] "The first and most gifted of creatures" (M'Swiney, *Psalms and Canticles,* 1901, p. 644).

[5] Perhaps in default of better explanation the "earth" verse may have been put into the third person in order to mark the transition from things celestial to those terrestrial.

The tendency of the arrangement of the Song proper is to descend from generals to particulars. It has a refrain at the end of each verse, slightly differing in those preliminary verses which are addressed to the Lord Himself, and wanting in the last three. The rendering of the refrain in the preliminary verses does not seem very happy in its English (A.V. and K.V.).

TITLE AND POSITION.

TITLE.

Forming, as it does, an integral portion of the third chapter of the Greek Daniel, the principal MSS. give the Song, in that place, no independent title. It falls of course under the general title of the whole Book, Daniel.

Van Ess in his LXX (Lips. 1835) entitles it Προσευχὴ Ἀζαρίου καὶ ὕμνος τῶν τριῶν, but as he puts this heading in curved brackets it is possibly merely his own insertion. 'B' is the codex which he is professing to follow in his text; but that MS. is credited with no such title in Dr. Swete's Greek Old Testament; nor do Holmes and Parsons shew any knowledge of it as existing in any of their MSS.

In the Veronese Graeco-Latin Psalter it is headed Ὕμνος τῶν πατέρων ἡμῶν, and in the Turin Psalter Ὕμνος τῶν τριῶν παιδῶν, which title it inserts again at v. 57, strangely regarding that verse as the commencement of a fresh canticle with a new number, ιβ. Churton (*Uncan. and Apocr. Script.*, p. 391) suggests that the former title "may have been wrongly transferred from Ecclus. xliv." at the head of which it stands. He also calls it the title in the Alexandrian Psalter—the Odes, presumably that is, at the end. But the title to Ecclus. xliv. is simply πατέρων ὕμνος, so that the likelihood of the transfer, deemed possible by Churton, having taken place is very small.

In the Odes, at the end of Cod. A, two canticles are extracted from this piece; the first (Ode IX.) entitled Προσευχὴ Ἀζαρίου, the second (Ode X.) Ὕμνος τῶν πατέρων ἡμῶν, each corresponding with the name given to it. In the office of Eastern Lauds the two parts have separate titles, being assigned to different days of the week (*D.C.A.* art. *Canticle*).

In the Syriac and Arabic versions of Daniel a separate title is given after v. 23 of chap. iii., and in the latter after v. 52, according to Churton in his marginal notes. He also says that "the prayer of the companions of *Ananias*" is the Syriac title. The titles on the whole are fairly suited to their purpose; but the use of the word "children" (παιδῶν) in the common heading of the Song contemplates the three as of the age indicated in Daniel i. rather than that in Daniel iii.

POSITION.

Obviously this is not meant for an independent work, since it has no proper commencement of its own. "And they walked" is clearly intended as a continuation of some foregoing history. Accordingly, its position in the LXX, Theodotion, Vulgate, and other versions, is immediately after the 23rd verse of Daniel iii., thus forming a portion of that chapter. This is clearly its natural and appropriate place. It unites well both at the beginning and the end with the canonical text, "Qui se trouve entrelassée (*sic*) dans le texte," as D. Martin says in the heading of the book in his French version. T.H. Home, however (*Introd.* 1856, II. 936), mentions its "abrupt nature" as a reason for thinking that the translator did not invent it, but made use of already existing materials. But the abruptness is not so apparent to other eyes and ears. Indeed G. Jahn, in his note on Dan. iii. 24 (Leipzig, 1904), considers the gap between vv. 23

and 24 in the Massoretic text is filled up satisfactorily in the LXX and Theodotion only.

By means of this insertion, and the inclusion of what in A.V. are the first four verses of chap. iv., this chapter is lengthened out in the Greek and Latin versions to exactly 100 verses.

Bishop Gray's note (*Key to O.T.* 1797, p. 608), in which he says "the Song of the three holy children is not in the Vat. copy of the LXX," is certainly a mistake. It is just possible, however, that he may have meant that the true LXX version was absent from it. So Ball somewhat obscurely (p. 310 "the Alex. MS. omits"[6]), and Bissell (p. 442), though not very distinctly, suggest a like idea as to its omission from Dan. iii. in A, and Zöckler in his commentary falls into the same mistake (Munich, 1891, p. 231). It is not unlikely that these writers successively influenced each other.

[6] This may refer to the titles he gives from "the Vatican LXX"; but see above, p. 18, as to the absence of these.

E. Philippe's idea (Vigouroux, *Dict.* II. 1267a), that this piece was separated from the original book because "elle retarde le récit et est en dehors du but final" seems unconvincing—as much so as Dereser's (quoted in Bissell, p. 444), from whom perhaps it was borrowed—that "the Sanhedrim at Jerusalem shortened it for convenient use," An equally unsatisfying "reason" is that of H. Deane in *Daniel, his Life and Times*, p. 70 (pref. 1888). "There is no doubt as to the antiquity of this addition, but probably on account of the feelings of hatred the three children express with regard to their enemies, it was not universally received by the Church." In the face of many stronger expressions in the O.T. received without hesitation, this explanation seems untenable, or at least insufficient. And the same may be said of G. Jahn's theory that some mention of the singing of the three, contained in the original, was expunged by the Massoretes as too wonderful and apocryphal.

Much has been made of the omission of this and the other additions from the original Syriac (*e.g.* Westcott, quoting Polychronius, Smith's *D.B.*, ed. 2. 7136, Bissell, 448), but they are contained in the Syriac text of Origen's *Hexapla*, in the MS. in the Ambrosian Library at Milan (Kautzsch, I. 172), published in facsimile by Ceriani. Bugati in his edition of Daniel gives this Syriac and the LXX text in parallel columns. In Jephet Ibn All's (the Karaite's) Arabic commentary on Daniel, translated by D.S. Margoliouth (Oxf. 1889), no notice is taken of the additions. The commentary was probably written about A.D. 1000.

Professor Rothstein (Kautzsch, I. 173) compares the situation of the prayer in ix. 4 *sqq.*, which he deems, like this one, to have been perhaps a later insertion into the book.

It is beyond question that if this psalm of prayer and praise is to find a place anywhere in the Book of Daniel, no more suitable position can be found for it than that which it occupies so well in the Greek. If it is a digression from the course of the original narrative it is very happily placed, since it accounts satisfactorily for the statement "the king was astonied" in v. 24 (91). He was surprised at the voice of praise, instead of the shrieks of pain which he had expected to produce by the execution of his decree.

AUTHORSHIP.

In the Greek of neither O´ nor Θ is there variation sufficient to prove that the writer differed from the one who translated the rest of the book. Rather do the indications point to the same hand having been at work throughout. Comely says of this and its companion pieces, "Neque in trium pericoparum argumentis quidquam invenitur quo illas Danielis auctori attribuere prohibeamur" (*Compendium,* Paris, 1889, p. 421). This, like other R.C. writings, holds of course a brief for their canonicity.

The Prayer, on the surface, claims to be by Azarias; the Song by all the three. The introductory and intermediate narrative verses are given as if from the same pen as the rest of Daniel's history; v. 4 (27) reminds us in its terms of Daniel iv. 37 (34) very strongly, and, in part, of ix. 14. In v. 24 (47) the mention of 49 (7 x 7) is paralleled by the symbolic use of the number 7 in iv. 25, etc. But even if, as is likely, they did not originate with the ostensible utterers, still it is quite possible that the hand for the prayer, the narrative, and the Song may not, in the first instance, have been identical.

Probably, however, we are intended, by the producer of the piece in its present shape, to understand that the prayer and the Song are recorded, even if not originated, by the author of the whole book. If not genuine parts of Daniel, their parentage has not been assigned to any named author; and the work must be treated as anonymous, for no clue has been traced which points to a definite writer.

The putting forward in v. 2 (25) of the second person of the trio, not otherwise distinguished from his fellows, is remarkable, and not suggestive of a forgery. There is nothing to shew why he led the prayer, as no special characteristics are attached to Abed-nego in our knowledge. Most likely a forger would have put the prayer into the mouth of Shadrach (Ananias), who always stands first, though the order of the last two is reversed in the one place in which the three are named in the uncanonical portion of the chapter. Ewald (*Hist. of Israel,* E. Tr. Lond. 1874, V. 486) thinks that Azarias is introduced as the eldest, or perhaps the teacher, of the other two; but this conjecture does not account for the varying orders of the names of the three in v. 65.

However thick a veil may rest over the author's name, it may safely be regarded as certain that he was a Jew, and a Jew who was well acquainted with the Psalter. But the opinion as to whether he was of Babylonian, Palestinian, or Alexandrian extraction will depend in a great measure on the view taken as to the original language, whether Chaldee, Hebrew, or Greek. Professor Rothstein (p. 174) admits the possibility of this addition having been made to Daniel before its translation into Greek. But Dean W.R.W. Stephens (*Helps to Study of P.B.*, Oxf. n. d., prob. 1901, p. 45) may be taken as representing what has been the commonest view. He thinks it "probably composed by an Alexandrine Jew." On the other hand, Dr. Streane's remark tells against this increase of contents having begun at Alexandria. "The tendency to diffuseness, characteristic of later Judaism... operated much more slightly among Egyptian Jews than with their brethren elsewhere" (quoted in Dr. Swete's *Introd. to Greek O.T.*, p. 259).

The assertion has gone the round of the commentators that the Song proper is a mere expansion of Psalm cxlviii., leaving us to infer that it is hardly a work of independent authorship. Perowne[7] writes, "the earliest imitation of this psalm is the Song of the Three Children." And J.H. Blunt, *in loc.*, tells us that "the hymn in its original shape was obviously an expanded form of the 148th Psalm." So even Gaster, "modelled evidently on Ps. cxlviii."[8]; while Wheatley[9] goes so far as to say that it is "an exact paraphrase" of that psalm, "and so like it in words and sense that whoever despiseth this reproacheth that part of the canonical writings."[10] But though the general idea for calling upon nature to glorify God is the same, the author of *Benedicite* is much more than a mere expander or imitator. Naturally many of the same objects are mentioned; but while comparison with the LXX version of the psalm shews some resemblance in word and thought, it shews much more variation in style, phraseology, and treatment. That the writer, as a Jew, was acquainted with this psalm can scarcely be doubted; that he consciously imitated it there is little to shew. Moreover, the use of this psalm at Lauds in the Ambrosian, the Eastern, and Quignon's service-books, together with the *Benedicite*, would hardly have occurred if the Church had regarded the latter as a mere expansion of the former, and not as a distinct production.

[7] *Psalms*, Lond. 1871, II. 462.

[8] *Proc. Soc. Bibl. Archæol.* 1895, p. 81.

[9] *Rational ittuitrat. of P.B.*

[10] But J.T. Marshall (Hastings' *D.B.* IV. 755), "The hymn is modelled after Ps. 136, and has equal claim to be considered poetical."

Whoever the author may have been, he was evidently strictly orthodox, and quite in sympathy with his three heroes, in whose mouths he placed this lively, agreeable, and most religious Song. He has added a much appreciated treasure, at least among Christians, to the ecclesiastical hooks; a most serviceable form of utterance for the Church's praiseful voice. But the nature of the piece does not afford much scope for display of the character or personality of the writer. He effaces himself while extolling devotion to Jehovah, and, if he be Daniel, while recording the faithfulness of the blessed friends of his youth. What subject more likely to excite his enthusiastic sympathy? Honour to the martyrs who endured, praise to the Lord who delivered, it was plainly a pleasure to him to give.

DATE AND PLACE.

DATE.

Almost everything, excepting its absence from the original, points to the Song having been from the beginning a part of the LXX text of Daniel. Its date therefore in this case would be the date of that text. The way in which it is worked into the canonical Daniel narrative suggests that, if there be any variation as to date in the three additions, this is seemingly the earliest.

That the LXX translator invented this enlargement out of his own genius seems highly improbable; nor, were it not for its absence from the original Daniel, few would have doubted that he obtained the whole of his material from the same quarter. In such case our 'apocryphon' would obviously ante-date the LXX text.

It is not unlikely that the Alexandrian translator worked up certain traditions (J.M. Fuller, S.P.C.K. *Comm.*; see also Bevan, *Dan.* Camb. 1892, p. 45), or, if Gaster's discovery be what he thinks, written narratives. What sources, however, were used in preparing its LXX Greek form can only be conjectured, and that on very slender data.

Rothstein in Kautzsch (I. 176) deems it to have been imported into the text of Daniel before the LXX translation, which he dates at latest in the first quarter of the last century B.C.

How an interpolation of this kind came to be admitted into the original of Daniel is a difficult matter to explain. Even on the supposition that the כתובים were less rigidly fixed than the Law or even the Prophets, the insertion or omission of such a section as this seems a very bold step. Ewald (*Hist. Israel,*

v. 86, 87, Eng. Tr.) thinks these additions to be fragments of an enlarged Daniel based on the older book, which was composed one or two centuries earlier.[11] Some later writer must have compared this new book, which was originally written in Greek, with the translation of the older book of Daniel, and transferred whatever he thought proper from the former into the latter. The work, thus compiled afresh, has been preserved in Greek shape, while the intervening book, whose former existence is proved by clearest traces, is now lost. It is only in this way, Ewald thinks, that we can explain the origin and preservation of the portions which are not contained in the Hebrew.

[11] He appears, on p. 303, to date Daniel between 160 and 170 B.C.

Prof. Kautzsch (I. 121) deems III. Maccabees, in vi. 6 of which book there is a reference to v. 27 (50) of the Song, to date from some time between the end of the second century B.C. and 70 A.D. at the latest. Within these limits he fixes upon the commencement of the Christian era as the most likely time. Dr. Streane, moreover (*Age of Macc.* p. 157), thinks that while century I. B.C. is very possible, it cannot be of earlier date, on account of the proof given by this verse of acquaintance with the Song. This reference, therefore, undoubted as it is, does not greatly help us in solving the problem of date, except as to its *ad quem* limit.

Tob. xii. 6 and xiii. 10 (the latter especially in the Vulgate) are very similar in phraseology to the refrain of the *Benedicite*; vv. 29, 30 (52) too, in both Greek versions, strongly suggest an acquaintance with Tob. viii. 5, since χύριε appears more likely to have been added to, than omitted from, the later document of the two. This is on the assumption that Tobit is, as Streane thinks (p. 148), pre-Maccabean, or at any rate earlier than this Song. But as the words used are not very distinctive, it is quite possible that they might have been independently prepared. The mention of Ananias, Azarias, and Misael in I. Macc. ii. 59 is not conclusive as to its writer's knowledge of the Song, but the order of the names, which does not occur elsewhere, makes a remembrance of v. 88 not improbable. I. Macc. is dated by Kautzsch (I. 31) from 100 to 90 B.C.; Streane (p. 149) allows slightly wider limits; and Westcott (Smith's *D.B.* II. 173) suggests 120 to 100. As to another possible indication given by v. 66 (88), see 'Chronology,' p. 69.

Of that scepticism which followed the refinements of rabbinism there is no trace, either here, or in Susanna, or in Bel and the Dragon. The tone of them all is that of an earlier time, free from any symptoms of this later decline. But still the signs of date are not sufficiently decided to justify us in fixing upon a narrow period with any degree of certainty. Taking the piece as independent of the original Daniel, the second century B.C. might perhaps be named as far from improbable. But a closer date than this it is hardly safe to fix.

If we assume an *Aramaic original*, Babylonia most probably will be the place for its production; Palestine somewhat less probably. But indications of place in the piece itself are very faint. It is true, however, that the order "nights and days" is "in conformity with the Shemitic custom of fixing the beginning of the day at the preceding evening" (McSwiney, *Psalms and Canticles*, 1901, p. 644).

Everyone must have noticed the frequency with which things watery and things cold are mentioned in the Song. The number of times they occur seems quite out of proportion with the scale on which it is conceived. Water, showers, dew, cold, frost, snow,[12] sea, rivers, fountains, all that move in the waters, are apostrophised in succession. The preponderance of these objects is very noticeable, even to a cursory reader. Now both Babylon and Alexandria are alike situated in hot countries; but of the two, a resident in the former would be more likely to have had these things brought before his eyes than a resident in the latter. Lower Egypt with its almost rainless climate, and its one river, does not seem the most likely locality to suggest a constant reference to such topics. Chaldæa, on the other hand, is better watered and is within the region of rain, and at any rate in its northern parts, of frost and snow. Dura, according to Keith Johnston's map, is close to the hills. But the position of "the plain of Dura," where the martyrdom took place, has not been certainly identified. J.M. Fuller's note on v. 42 (64), "Rain and dew have that prominence which naturally belongs to them in the parched East," is far from sufficing to explain the oft recurring mention of these matters.

[12] This particularly is unsuggestive of Egypt.

Still less does Bishop Forbes' remark[13] that "the element of water seems specially to have received the benediction of the Lord," serve to elucidate the cause of its preponderance here.

[13] *Commentary on Canticles in Divine Service*, Lond. 1853, p. 81.

The slight anthropomorphism in v. 54, where 'sitting' is implied in Θ, expressed in O', is more conformable to Babylonian than Alexandrian ideas; but this may be a mere reminiscence of Psalms lxxx. 1, xcix. 1. The mention of pitch or bitumen is inconclusive, inasmuch as it is found in both Babylonia and Egypt; but the mention of "heavens" and "stars of heaven" (vv. 59, 63), agrees very well with Chaldean origin. So far, therefore, as these considerations go, they turn the scale, to a small extent, in favour of Babylonia.

The only natural object which may be regarded as telling in the opposite direction is κήτη (v. 79), which might be thought to point to knowledge of the Mediterranean Sea (*see* Child Chaplin, *Benedicite*, 1879, p. 324).

The birthplace of the LXX text is surely Alexandria. The character of this, as of the other additions, indicates, according to Westcott (*D.B.* ed. 2, I. 1714a) and Wordsworth (on Dan. iii. 23), the hand of an Alexandrian writer.

It is well, however, to notice that this, with its companion pieces, has as few indications of Greek philosophy and habits of thought as any part of the Apocrypha; and in common with most Alexandrian writers it has little or nothing of purely Egyptian character. Still, Dereser's idea that "Daniel may have written his book in Greek at Babylon with all the additions" (quoted by Bissell, p. 444) seems most unlikely, and could hardly have been advanced except under the necessity of supporting the Roman view of the book.

Theodotion's version, so far as concerns the locality where it originated, shares the obscurity which hangs over much of Theodotion's personal life. Ephesus may be suggested, for Irenæus (III. xxiii.) styles him ὁ Ἐφέσιος; though Epiphanius calls him Ποντικός (*D.C.B.* art. *Hexapla*, p. 22a). The latter author is, for the most part, the less accurate of the two. In *De Mensuris, etc.*, XVII. he states that Θ's version was issued in the second Commodus' reign, 180-192, "obviously too late."[14] The pre-Theodotionic version which Θ is thought to have used may of course have been an Alexandrian production; but at present little is known of it.

[14] Swete, *Introd. to Greek O.T.*, p. 43.

That Theodotion had some earlier rendering, besides the LXX as his basis, the quotations in Rev. ix. 20, etc., and St. Matt. xii. 18, coinciding with his version,[15] render highly probable, inasmuch as he wrote subsequently to any likely date for those books. Possibly he may have used Aquila's version, or that of some unknown translator. Professor Gwynn's idea (*D.C.B.* art. *Theodotion*, 977a) of "two rival Septuagintal Daniels"[16] seems to have more "inherent improbability" than he is inclined to admit. But where this ground text, circulated apparently in Palestine and Asia Minor, was made, who can say? But if we take St. John as the author of Revelation, his connection with Ephesus, and the probable publication of his work there, give some little support to the theory of an Ephesian origin of Theodotion's translation.

[15] *Op. cit.*, pp. 48, 396, 403.

[16] *Cf.* Ewald in 'Date,' p. 29.

It is strange that a version supposed to be made by one who was not an orthodox Christian, if Christian at all, should have been preferred, as far as concerns Daniel, by the Christian Church for ordinary use.[17] Jerome (*Præf. in Dan.*) says, as if he felt that some explanation was needed, "et hoc cur acciderit nescio," though he proceeds to suggest some possible reasons why the version of one "qui utique post adventum Christi incredulus fuit" should have been so much honoured. The religious work of a Jew, who lived before Christ, and that of one who refused to acknowledge his advent after it had taken place, stand obviously, for Christians, on a different footing.

[17] Some slight warrant, or at least precedent, for using our R.V., in which dissenters had a hand, might perhaps be found in this fact.

FOR WHOM AND WITH WHAT OBJECT WRITTEN.

FOR WHOM.

Undoubtedly for Jewish readers, who were already interested in the story of Shadrach, Meshach, and Abed-nego; designed for those who had Daniel's book in their hands, who felt the Three to be heroes rightly honoured.

Of course, if the words were really spoken by Azarias, they were for the honour of God and the benefit of himself and his companions in the fire; and the Song itself becomes a real thanksgiving, on the spur of the moment, for the literal fulfilment of such promises as Isai. xliii. 2—a form, for their own personal use, to express their immediate feelings.

Verse 24 (O´) might suggest the idea that the prayer (and perhaps the Song also) were uttered in the interval between the issue and the execution of the king's order for burning alive; but the words ἐν μέσῳ τῷ πυρί in v. 25 forbid this view. (As to a possible subsequent insertion of the prayer, see 'Integr. and State of Text,' p. 42.) Theodotion also precludes this idea by his insertion of ἐν μέσῳ τῆς φλογὸς in v. 24 itself, as well as ἐν μέσῳ τοῦ πυρὸς in v. 25. The slight change in the case of the last two words lessens the likelihood of their having been transferred from v. 25 of one version to v. 25 of the other. But it is quite possible that Θ may have purposely omitted the clause in v. 24 of O´, beginning ὅτε αὐτοὺς, in order to shut out the idea of these devotions having taken place in the interval suggested above.

Dean Farrar even says that the Song is "not very apposite" (*Expositor's Bible*, Daniel, Lond. 1895, p. 180), though other minds find it remarkably so. In writing on v. 27 (50) he erroneously substitutes νότιον for δρόσον. This is probably copied from Ball's note *in loc.* If the latter part of v. 66 (88) was in the original Song, the reference to their own position is of course apposite enough.

Even a writer of such a stamp as Albert Barnes (*Comm. on Dan.* iii. 23) is obliged to confess that "with some things that are improbable and absurd, the Song contains many things that are beautiful and that would be highly appropriate if a song had been uttered at all in the furnace." But to a contrary effect J. Kennedy goes even further than Dean Farrar, calling it "an elaborate composition by some one whose imagination failed to realise what was fitting and natural to men in the position of the three Hebrews in the fiery furnace" (*Dan. from a Christian Standpoint*, 1898, p. 55).

The passage vv. 26 to 34 is provided in Littledale's *Priest's P.B.* (1876, p. 95) as a suitable Scripture reading for those "in fever." Although there is a kind of appropriateness in the narrative of the fire being driven off, many would regard this application of the extract as highly fanciful, and not quite agreeable to the object with which the piece was written.

OBJECT.

Unless we assume the writer to be purely an imaginative novelist, the preservation of serviceable traditions as profitable records of religion, is clearly his principal aim. This addition cannot reasonably be said in any way to distort or disagree with, though it adds to, the sacred narrative. It is very well fitted into the main story; and the non-appearance of Daniel is quite in accord with his absence from the scene in chap. iii.

An edifying purpose is most conspicuous, and, if we assume that it is really an interpolation of the original book, we may well suppose with Bishop Gray, that "some writer desirous of imitating and embellishing the sacred text" has left us this specimen of his work; that the veneration of some Hellenistic Jew probably induced him to fabricate this ornamental addition to the history (*op. cit.* pp. 610, 611).

One aim would be to satisfy the interest awakened by the wonderful experiences of the three, which afforded a narrative ground-work for this extension; falling in this respect, as Prof. Ryssel points out (Kautzsch I. 167), into the same category as the Prayer of Manasses and the additions to Esther. It may be said that resistance to idolatry, securing divine deliverance, is, as in Bel and the Dragon, the "motif" of the piece. But this is not accomplished without great peril and anxiety to these martyrs in will, who kept before them an uncompromising standard, worthy of their noble lineage (Dan. i. 3), as well as of their true religion.

In some respects we are reminded of Jonah's prayer, which had a similar object, viz., to secure a deliverance from hopeless danger, a deliverance as marvellous as that of the Three. The words by which it is introduced are similar (καὶ προςηύξατο Ἰωνᾶς... ἐκ τῆς κοιλίας τοῦ κήτους καὶ εἶπεν, Jon. ii. 2; καὶ συστὰς Ἀζαρίας προςηύξατο καὶ... ἐν μέςῳ τοῦ πυρὸς εἶπεν, Dan. iii. 25,

Θ); and the spirit of turning to God in dire straits is the same. But Jonah's prayer differs from Azarias' in containing much mention of his immediate danger. Yet the absence of this from Azarias' prayer hardly amounts to a probable indication of forgery; indeed the possibility of so long an utterance implies some restraint of the consuming power of the furnace, such as is described in v. 27 of the Chaldee.

A subsidiary purpose answered in the Song proper is that of joining nature with ourselves, by addressing it in a series of invitations to magnify Him who is its God and ours alike, thus interpreting the feelings which nature maybe supposed to entertain. It is recognised that the irrational as well as the rational have their rightful spheres of action; and a wholesome sympathy is manifested with those portions of nature—which we think are lower than ourselves. With this may be compared Adam and Eve's morning hymn (in Milton's *Paradise Lost*, Book V., 1. 153 *sq.*), which is very similar in tone and in sequence of objects apostrophized.

The Song so readily leads itself to use as a Canticle that the idea inevitably arises of its having been composed with that purpose in view; but proof that it was ever so used by the Jews seems entirely wanting. The statements made in some P.B. manuals that it was so used appear to have arisen from a misunderstanding of an ambiguous sentence of Wheatley's (*see* 'Liturgical Use,' p. 83). Still, there may have been an *arrière pensée* in the composer's mind of providing models of prayer and of praise for others, in crisis of trial or deliverance, to offer unto God. It is pleasing to note in this respect, that the thanksgiving is not stinted, but is even longer than the prayer. Nowhere is the manifold wealth of God's revelation in nature more fully and comprehensively set forth in the most exalted spirit of praise; so that, if this were one of the composer's objects, it is most abundantly answered.

INTEGRITY AND STATE OF THE TEXT.

It has been suggested by Prof. Rothstein (in Kautzsch I. 174, 175) that the prayer of Azarias, the intermediate narrative, and the Song itself, were not all written at the same time. But this view is based purely on internal probability, and derives little or no support from any of the MSS. or versions, unless the introduction of titles in the Arabic after v. 28 (51), and in some Greek copies to the prayer of Azarias, be thought to give it countenance; yet these may have crept in from their convenience for liturgical use, and so be accounted for merely on practical grounds.

To base this separation, however, on a supposed disagreement between v. 15 (38) and vv. 31 (53), 62 (84), is certainly insufficient cause, as Ball points out (307b), for assigning Prayer and Song to different writers (*see* 'Chronology,'

p. 67). But the observation that the narrative passage between the Prayer and the Song fits in well after the canonical v. 23[18] seems a stronger basis for supposing that the prayer is a later introduction than the Song. Rothstein points out (p. 181, note d) that v. 1 (24) in Θ has relation to the Song, but not to the Prayer, and originally, as he imagines, took the place of the present v. 28 (91) of similar import. Corn. a Lap. notes of v. 1 (24) "est hysterologia." This view is also mentioned with favour in Charles' article on Apocrypha in the 1902 vols. of *Encycl. Brit.* (*cf.* 'For whom written,' p. 36).

[18] G. Jahn in his "restoration" of the Hebrew text of Daniel from the LXX, admits vv. 28 and 49-51 into his canonical text (Leipzig, 1904).

It is observable also that the statement of v. 26 (48) is not a mere repetition of that in v. 22, but refers to the scorching of the onlookers, while v. 22 speaks of those who executed the king's order.[19]

[19] As to the possibility of the fact, *cf. Yorkshire Post*, April 12th, 1902, on Coronation bonfires: "Spectators should keep clear of the lee side. The flame of such bonfires has been known to stream in a flash 150ft. out."

The repetition of the same invocation at the commencement of the Prayer and the Song is noteworthy; if the two are not contemporary, it has probably been borrowed by the composer of the Prayer. But the difficulty (often magnified) of reconciling the statements of v. 15 (38) with the Jews' civil and ecclesiastical condition at the time of Daniel iii. wears quite a different aspect if the Prayer is regarded as an interpolation of later date by another hand. Altogether this theory of the interpolation of the Prayer is surrounded with a considerable air of probability.

Five extra verses are interspersed in the Syriac of the Song, calling upon the hosts of the Lord, ye that fear the Lord, cold and heat (the winter and summer of our *Benedicite*), the herbs of the field, and the creeping things of the earth (Churton's translation). Of these "frigus and aestus" is in the Vulgate, taken from Θ. The source of the others is unapparent, though creeping things would very naturally follow beasts and cattle, as in Gen. vii. 14.

The present ending of the Song, after the usual refrain in the middle of v. 66 (88) is of a laboured nature with a decidedly "dragging" style. It certainly has the appearance of being an afterthought, added by some not very skilful composer, who fancied the original termination to be too abrupt, and thought he could attach an appropriate supplement. But of this theory no external evidence is at present forthcoming.

Θ agrees with the O′ text much more closely in this than in the other additions. Most verses are the same, word for word; and many others have but the slightest variations. He makes a few small omissions, as in (Greek)

vv. 24, 40, 67, 68; but in general he follows O´ exactly. Even vv. 67, 68, are contained in A, in both places, in Daniel and in the Odes at the end; also they are in the Turin Psalter, though omitted in the Veronese (Swete's LXX). As they are found, with a little difference in the O´ text, they may have fallen out of B and Q accidentally. The identical refrain at the end of each verse would naturally facilitate an error of this kind.

The principal MSS. available for Θ's text are the same as those for the canonical part of Daniel, A, B, and Q. Γ fails us here, as in other passages, except from vv. 37-52, in which its variations are unimportant.

Taking B as the ground-work, A's changes are not generally of serious moment, excepting in the case of the two inserted verses, 67 and 68, and the transposition of vv. 73 and 74. Otherwise they chiefly consist of small insertions or omissions which do not materially affect the sense (vv. 36, 81); varying forms from the same root such as ὑπεραινετός for αἰνετός (v. 54), εὐλογημένος for εὐλογητός (v. 56). The correctors of B in v. 38, though unsupported by the chief codices, certainly seem right in substituting οὐδε for οὐ. Q's variations not unfrequently agree with A's; where they do not, they are scarcely more important, and often partake of a similar character. In v. 88 a synonym is substituted, viz., ἔσωσεν for ἐρύσατο (2nd). In the few verses covered by Γ, B is generally agreed with; a change of case, αὐτούς instead of αὐτοῖς, appearing in v. 50.

LANGUAGE AND STYLE.

LANGUAGE.

The probability of a Semitic original lying in the background of this piece, has always been considerable. Those who have maintained Greek as the original language, have generally spoken a little less confidently with regard to this than with regard to its two companion pieces. So Bissell writes (p. 443), though a supporter of the Greek (p. 43), "undoubtedly more can be said in favour of such a theory" [of a Semitic original] "than for a similar one in respect of the two remaining additions." And since M. Gaster discovered in 1894 an Aramaic text, the grounds for deeming the Greek to be the original, though not set aside, have been partially undermined. Schürer, however, in Hauck's *Encycl.* (I. 639), appears to think that this is translated from Θ, and not *vice versâ*, as Gaster claims. In his third German ed. of *H.J.P.* (III. 333) he agrees with Gaster in deeming תודוס to be Θ, but considers the Aramaic to be a rendering of Θ's Greek, taken into the tenth-century Chronicle of Jerahmeel.

It must be confessed that the existence of two Greek versions increases the probability, though it does not prove the existence, of an original in another language. It does not seem likely that Θ would have revised the O´ of the additions in the same way as the canonical part, unless he had a similar basis to go upon in both cases. If not, why, and on what authority, did he alter the additions at all? And this consideration applies to the other two, even more than to the one we are dealing with, inasmuch as the version of Susanna and of Bel and the Dragon involved more numerous changes. Irenæus' statement that Theodotion "ἡρμήνευσεν," taken strictly, would of course always imply an original to translate; but Irenæus may only have been thinking of the particular passage from Isaiah which he refers to (III. xxiii.).

Many phrases may be instanced which point to a Semitic original, or at least fit in well with the theory of its existence. Towards counterbalancing this there is a much smaller number which may be thought to tell in the opposite direction. But in the main, as Comely truly writes (*op. cit.* p. 420), "accedit hebraismorum frequentia quum in Alexandrini tum in Theodotionis versione."[20]

[20] Dr. Julian (*Dict. Hymnol.* p. 134) has the following strange sentence as to *Benedicite*, " It is not in the Hebrew version (*sic*) of the Scriptures, and on this ground, among others, it is omitted from A.V."

It is to be observed, however, that the names of the Three are Grecized from their original Hebrew nomenclature,[21] although their Babylonian names are employed in Dan. iii., and adopted by O´ and Θ in the canonical portions, both before and after the apocryphal episode. An apparent exception occurs in v. 23 of O´, where clauses of that verse and of v. 22 have been transposed and slightly altered. Here Azarias occurs in the same form as in the apocryphal portion. But this isolated use of the Hebrew form of his name has probably been brought about by the insertion of our piece into the chapter, the same form and phrase, τοῖς περὶ τὸν Ἀζαρίαν, being found in v. 49 of both Greek texts. A like phrase occurs in Ezek. xxxviii. 6, and in Acts xiii. 13. The order of names, too, differs in this Addition from their order elsewhere, the two last changing places, thus bringing Azarias (Abed-nego) into the middle. It is remarkable that he is twice, vv. 2 (25) and 8 (49), placed as if he were the leading member of the trio, in the former verse as uttering the prayer, in the latter as heading the party in the furnace; and so also, as pointed out above, in v. 23 of O´. This last fact, however, is counterbalanced in the same version by all three being named in v. 24 as praying, Azarias not there figuring as the sole speaker. These small indications certainly point to some ancient distinction between the uncanonical insertion, as we have it, and the body of the book.

E. Philippe (in Vigouroux' *D.B.* II. p. 1266) argues for Hebrew and not Greek originals, because of the existence of two Greek versions, neither of which, he says, appears to be a revision of the other, containing hebraisms suggestive of a Hebrew original. But as regards the Song of the Three, this statement, that neither version is a revision of the other, must be regarded as more than doubtful. He also says that the Chisian and Syro-Hexaplar MSS. contain critical signs of Origen, revealing a Hebrew text, and in 87 (Chisianus) at xiii. 1-5, A´, Σ´, Θ´ indicate Aquila, Symmachus, and Theodotion, all translators from the Hebrew. This last point, however, may not stand as to the Song of the Three (*see* note in Kautzsch, p. 176) so far as Aquila is concerned. For Origen, in his letter to Africanus, seems to imply that Aquila's rendering did not contain the Song: Οὕτω γὰρ Ἀκύλας δουλεύων τῇ Ἑβραικῇ λεξει ἐκδέδωκεν—§ 2.

Jerome's words in the Vulgate, after v. 23, "quæ sequuntur in Hebraeis voluminibus non reperi," are very guarded, not absolutely denying the existence of a Hebrew text, but merely asserting that he has not met with it. Cod. Amiatinus, however, has 'non repperiuntur,' an expression which asserts more comprehensively the absence of this passage in his time.

The following are some specific indications of language which appear to be of sufficient interest to be noted separately:

v. 27 O´, Θ. Δίκαιος εἶ ἐπὶ πᾶσιν = צַדִּיק צ rendered by ἐπὶ in Dan. ix. 14 (in both versions) and in Neh. ix. 33. Δίκαιος ἐπὶ also occurs in Bar. ii. 9, in that part of Baruch which is almost certainly a translation from the Hebrew. Ball (*Speaker's Comm.*) gives a similar phrase from the *Iliad*, and Bissell a still more apposite one from *Il.* IV. 28, to shew that it is not unknown in pure Greek. Gaster's Aramaic has simply ל not צ.

v. 30 O´, Θ. Ὑπακούω governs the genitive correctly, but συντηρέω, coupled with it, is made to govern the same noun. Exigencies of translation might easily cause this awkwardness, but hardly original Greek composition.

v. 31 O´. Καὶ νῦν = וְעַתָּה So translated in II. Chron. vi. 16, 17 at the beginning of the verse, as here; it occurs again in vv. 33 and 41 in both versions, as also in ix. 15, 17. It is not a very natural beginning of a Greek sentence.

v. 32 O´, Θ. Why ἀποστατῶν, a title which does not seem very applicable to the Babylonians? It may be merely a rendering of טרד as in Ezra iv. 12, 15.

The Vulgate here has 'prævaricator.' In Gaster's Aramaic the verse is different. But *cf.* use of ἀπηλλοτριωμένοι in Eph. ii. 12 of those who had never belonged to Israel.

v. 33 O´, Θ. Οὐκ ἔστιν ἡμῖν ἀνοῖξαι looks very like a translation of אֵין לָנוּ, an idiom used in II. Chron. xxxv. 3, 15 in the sense of 'cannot,' followed by a verb in the infinitive. *Cf.* Heb. ix. 5.

v. 34 O´, Θ. Εἰς τέλυς = לְכָלָה or לָנֶצַח as in II. Chron. xii. 12, Ps. xv. 11. Διασκεδάσης σου τὴν διαθήκην. This curious expression may be the rendering of such a phrase as that in I. Kings xv. 19, הָפֵרָה אֶת בְּרִיתְךָ, there translated by the same words; also in Jer. xi. 10.

v. 36 O´, Θ. Ἄστρα τοῦ οὐρανοῦ, as in viii. 10, xii. 3, both O´.

v. 37 O´, Θ. Ταπεινοὶ ἐν. Did the translators read בכל for מכל?

v. 38 O´, Θ. Καρπῶσαι. *Cf.* Lev. ii. 9, 11, קטר אשה being similarly translated. Καρπόω is also used in the same sense in I. Esd. iv. 52. Deissmann has an interesting 'study' of this word in his *Bible Studies* (Eng. transl., Edinb. 1901, p. 135).

v. 40 O´, Θ. Ἐνώπιον ... ὄπισθεν = לפני... אחרי. Ἐκτελέσαι is thought by Ball to have arisen from some confusion between כליל and כלל, but this is dubious. Marshall (Hastings' *D.B.* IV. 755b) suggests שלם in Kal or Piel.

v. 44 O´, Θ. Ἐνδικνύμενοι, Grotius (in *Critici Sacri*) says "Expressit Hebræum הראה quod est in Ps. lx. 3 (5) et alibi." The verb is so translated in Exod. ix. 16.

v. 49 O´, Θ. The apparent Grecism of οἱ περὶ τὸν Ἀζαρίαν occurs in the LXX of Ezek. xxxviii. 6 and elsewhere. Συγκατέβη ἅμα, Ball suggests ירד אחרי from Ps. xlix. 18. Gaster gives צם נחית. Ἐξετίναξε, Gaster characterises as a "senseless" rendering of ואיצטנין "and it cooled down," which word certainly gives an excellent sense.

v. 50 O´, Θ. The well known "crux" of πνεῦμα δρόσου διασυρίζον appears in the Aramaic as די מינשבא טלא כרוחא which Gaster translates "as a wind that blows (and causes) the dew (to descend)."

v. 51 O´. καὶ ἐγέντο = וַיְהִי.

v. 54 O´. Δόξης τῆς βασιλείας, *cf.* Dan. iv. 36 (33) Θ´, τιμὴν τῆς βασιλείας. יקר מלכות is the Aramaic in both places. θρόνου δόξης, as in Jer. xiv. 21. θρόνος is used of God's throne in Dan. vii. 9, end.

v. 59 O´, Θ. Οὐρανοί = שָׁמַיִם (not in Gaster's Aramaic).

vv. 64, 68 O´. Repetition of δρόσος, and vv. 67, 69 O´, of ψῦχος, suggests possible difficulty of a translator, causing him to fall back on same word.

vv. 65, 86 O´, Θ. The different senses of πνεύματα point to רוּחוֹת as the underlying original of both.

v. 87 O´, Θ. Ταπεινοὶ τῇ καρδίᾳ; Luther renders "elend und betrübt sind," since these words, if of literal and immediate application, would indicate the depression of the Babylonian exiles; and so would tell in favour of a Semitic original, Greek being unfamiliar to them.

v. 88 O´, Θ. Ἐκ μέσου καιομένης φλογός, cf. Dan. iii. 21, 29; vii. 11 (יקד, Chald. in first and third of these cases, and also in Gaster's Aramaic of this piece).

v. 89 O´, Θ. Ἐξείλετο does not seem a very suitable word, as they had not yet been into ᾅδης. It may be a translation of ישע as in Jer. xlii. 11, if from a Hebrew original. שיזבנא is given by Gaster as the original of both ἐξείλατο (Θ) and ἐρρύσατο.

v. 90 O´, Θ. Οἱ σεβόμενοι, used of proselytes of the gate in Acts xvii. 17, may have this meaning here also, as coming last, and in connection with τὸν θεὸν τῶν θεῶν, a possible reference to the "gods of the nations." Gaster's Aramaic has nothing answering to σβόμενοι. Grotius suggests "יראי אלהים ut Job i. I, 8, ii. 3," where θεοσεβής is the word.

The writer deems the evidence of language to point on the whole to a Semitic rather than to a Greek base. The difficulty of balancing the indications however of the original language is shewn by the names of important authorities which may be ranged on either side, Ball, Rothstein, and Swete regarding the Semitic as probable; Westcott, Schürer, and Fritzsche holding a similar opinion as to the Greek.

When a Semitic original is pronounced for, the further question arises, was it Hebrew or Aramaic? The grounds unfortunately appear too indecisive to warrant a distinct choice between these alternatives.

STYLE.

This is the only one of the three Additions which takes a devotional and poetical form. The Song has perhaps exceeded the others in the great estimation accorded to it. The frequent liturgical use made of it is both a sign and a cause of this.

The style of the Greek is Hellenistic, and is not out of character with the versions of which it is a part; nor in particular with the Book of Daniel with which it is incorporated. It is spirited, interesting, and agreeable, mainly Hebraic in the character of its thought and cast of its language.

The Prayer may possibly be accused of the needless repetition of similar sentiments; especially in vv. 4, 5, and 8 as to God's truth and justice; and in vv. 6 and 7 as to Israel's disobedience, which are somewhat over-insisted upon. But perhaps this may be attributed to earnest pleading. It is instructive to compare and contrast Daniel's Prayer, chap. ix., remembering that a different person would naturally have a different style; a consideration which may also help to account for the change we are conscious of when we pass from the prayer of Azarias to the Song which purports to he the composition of the Three.

The principle on which πᾶς is inserted in some verses and omitted in others does not seem clear. Rhythmical considerations do not sufficiently account for it. Something other than style seems to have influenced its use; but what that something may have been it is difficult to discern. Nor does the principle seem clearer in the Aramaic than in the Greek.

The poem has a simple yet majestic structure, with a refrain apt to linger in the ear, either in Greek or English, Εὐλογεῖτε, ὑμνεῖτε, καὶ ὑπρυψοῦτε αὐτὸν εἰς τοὺς αἰῶνας, "Bless ye the Lord, praise Him, and magnify Him for ever." In Gaster's Aramaic the refrain is slightly varied, לצלמא being used where God is addressed, בצלמא where His creatures are exhorted. Dr. Gaster understands the former to mean "for ever," but the latter "in the world."[22] This distinction, if a just one, is entirely obliterated in the versions. In the Vulgate however the refrain sounds less agreeably, for "superexaltate " is a cumbrous word for frequent repetition. It is one of those exaggerated compounds of which the translator of Daniel seems to have been too fond, such as "superlaudabilis," "supergloriosus" (v. 52), "deambulo" and "discoöperio" (Sus. vv. 8, 32). This inconvenience was evidently felt in liturgical use, as in the Roman Breviary and Missal the repetition of "superexaltate" is avoided. Psalm cxxxvi. affords a biblical instance of a refrain similarly repeated at the end of each verse; and Deut. xxvii. 15-26 may be regarded as containing a liturgical repetition of another species.

[22] *Proc. Sac. Bibl. Archæol.* 1895, p. 80.

The use of a symbolic multiple of 7 in v. 24 (47) accords well with a similar practice in Daniel iii. 19, ix. 24, and x. 2,13. The number 3 itself (v. 28) may also be symbolic; but this is merely continued from the canonical part of the story, being quite of a piece with it. No other numbers occur.

There is a remarkable resemblance between the natural objects mentioned in Ecclus. xliii. and in the Song. Especially v. 22[23] of the former is like v. 27 (50) of the latter in its leading idea. The furnace, κάμινος, is also named in v. 4 of the Ecclus. passage; and the aim of glorifying God is most prominent in both. But the resemblance in style to Psalm cxlviii. is not so great as has sometimes been imagined. (See what is said on this point under 'Authorship,' p. 26.) On the whole, the style of the work, whether supplicatory, narrative, or poetic, is well suited to the purpose for which it is designed; and although the influence of previous writers is evident, the manner of the author is not that of a mere imitator of their compositions. He has a form of his own in which to present his subject.

[23] In the Hebrew of this verse the parallel is less striking.

RELIGIOUS AND SOCIAL STATE.

RELIGIOUS.

So far as the Jewish actors in the scene are concerned, they exhibit a true religious spirit from the O.T. standpoint, with an unshakeable firmness of conviction that Jehovah alone should be worshipped.

The episode shews (in common with the canonical part) that the Captivity had already produced a stubborn opposition to idolatrous temptations among the Jews. The tendency to follow after other gods, and to depart from Jehovah in this way, had been outrooted from the habits of these exiles; and their example now would be for all time an incentive to others to resist, at any cost, the pressing inducements to become idolaters.

It is difficult to find anything really inconsistent with the religious position, so far as we know it, of Israel in Babylon. Bissell, however, writes strongly to the contrary, in company as he avers, with almost all non-Romish scholars. This opinion is based on little more than the supposed inappropriateness of the Prayer and Song to the occasion, and on the discrepancy of v. 15 (38) with the circumstances of the time, and with other parts of the composition (p. 445 and on v. 15). This "discrepancy" is dealt with under 'Chronology.' Bissell also quotes with approval the exaggerated comparison of Eichhorn, who deems the three "like dervishes gifted in penitential exclamations, which they interrupt by abuse of Nebuchadnezzar." A consistent religious ground is maintained throughout by the three; there is for them no "doing at Rome as Rome does" in vital matters of religion. And their condition is evidently compassionated by God, their faithfulness approved, amid the persecutions of a foreign land.

Considerable talent and art in devotional composition are manifested in confession, petition, and praise—talent and art of which the Christian Church has widely availed herself from a very early period. The tone of Azarias' prayer is not discordant with Daniel's description of his own prayer in ix. 20, nor with the prayer itself immediately preceding that verse, either in sentiment or phraseology. They may well have come from the same editor, whether the prime author of the whole book or not. Verse 16 (39) apparently contains phrases culled from Pss. xxxiv. 18, li. 17. M. Parker on Deut. xxviii. 56 (*Bibliotheca Biblica*, Oxf. 1735) thinks that the declaration of the three in v. 9 (32) corresponds with Deut. xxviii. 49, 50, being in fact a public acknowledgment that national impiety had brought upon them the distress in which they were at present involved. If so, it shews knowledge of the law on their part. But the connection is one solely of idea, and not of phraseology. There is a strong connection in phraseology, however, between v. 27 and Deut. xxxii. 4 in LXX. In any case the religious tone of the whole production is not inconsistent with what we might have expected.

SOCIAL.

The nature of this piece does not afford much scope for the display of the social condition of Babylon and its inhabitants. It is to be expected therefore that it will shew us far less of these matters than either Susanna or Bel and the Dragon. But so far as it gives any indications, it is in accord with the canonical Daniel, and with what we know from other sources of the customs of the country. Evidently Israel was in a state of subjection to the Babylonian king, who ordered idolatry to be practised by captives and natives alike. It is shewn by v. 9 (32) *sqq.* that the former smarted under his tyranny, and appealed to God for redress, like their forefathers in Egyptian bondage.

The punishment of burning, on which the whole story turns, is quite Babylonian. Jer. xxix. 22 is another instance, so that there is no lack of *vraisemblance* in its introduction here. (*See* Hastings' *D.B.* art. *Crimes and Punishments*, I. 523, for other instances). It has been thought (Smith's *D.B.* ed. 2 art. *Furnace*, I. 1092b) that this furnace in Daniel is alluded to by our Lord in St. Matt. xiii. 42, 50; but how opposite on this occasion are the consequences of being cast into it! Here prayer and praise from the righteous, there weeping and gnashing from the wicked. The allusion must be considered a very doubtful one.

The subservience of the king's servants[24] in performing their cruel work, and the absence of a protesting voice or of a helping hand from any quarter, is very characteristic of the results of Eastern despotism. All, except the three martyrs, were afraid of Nebuchadnezzar, whose murderous rage under contradiction is of a piece in both the Chaldee and the Greek portions of the chapter. No one else on this occasion dared to disobey his decree, and there is no sign of anyone venturing so much as to intercede for the Jewish victims.

[24] ὑπηρέται, v. 23 (46), attendants probably holding some official position superior to that of slaves. *Cf.* St. John xviii. 18.

In such small glimpses as are given, in this extension of chap. iii., of the social state of Babylonia there is nothing clearly indicating that the interpolation (if such it be) is of an unhistoric or untrustworthy character, nothing wholly irreconcilable with the rest of the book. Indeed the author (W.T. Bullock) of the note on Daniel iii. 23 in the S.P.C.K. *Commentary* goes so far as to write of "that noble canticle *Benedicite*," as an "historical document." This expression may require qualification, but it is not beyond the bounds of possible fact.

THEOLOGY.

The theology appears to be of a perfectly orthodox character, quite what might have been expected from the three children; nor is it inconsistent with that contained in the rest of the book of Daniel. The exile had not now contaminated the Jewish religion, but had rather purged it of its corruptions, and eradicated in particular the fatal tendency to "serve other gods." Such sins are thoroughly confessed by Azarias in a style not without resemblance to Daniel's confession. (*Cf.* v. 6 (29) with ix. 5 in both versions; also Esther xiv. 6, 7.)

The God of their fathers is He alone to whom prayers and praises are to be addressed. He is regarded as the Lord of all creation, both as a whole and in its specific parts. He is looked up to to make good the old promises (13), being full of mercy (19), as well as of power and glory (20, 22, 68). He is a king (33), just (4), and gracious (67), with an ear open to the addresses of his people. The righteousness of even His heavy judgements is acknowledged in the prayer; and the hymn throughout shews that the gratitude of man is plainly deemed acceptable to Him.

As to the question of praise being called for from inanimate things or irrational beings, we must remember that though unfitted, so far as we understand them, for conscious praise, their creation, maintenance, and usefulness give evidence of God's greatness and goodness. As Cornelius à Lapide notes on v. 35 (57) "Inanimes creaturæ benedicunt Deum creatorem suum, non ore sed opere, ait S. Hieronymus," giving, however, no reference to the passage in Jerome. Ps. civ. 4 and Heb. i. 7 afford some helpful clues to the operations of Nature in this connection. Man is treated by our author as the interpreter of Nature, with a right, as made in the image of God, to call upon it to glorify its Maker. He offers vocal praise on its behalf as well as on his own; though things without life praise God silently, by fulfilling the parts for which He made them. A somewhat similar idea of the elevating influence exerted by natural beings may be discerned in the second of the *New sayings of Jesus* as restored by Messrs. Grenfell and Hunt (Lond. 1904, p. 15). And Addison fitly writes (*Spect.* No. 393), "The cheerfulness of heart which springs up in us from the survey of Nature's works, is an admirable preparation for gratitude "(*cf.* 'Early Christian Literature and Art,' *s.v.* 'Hippolytus').

Azarias desires that the rescue of the party may redound to the knowledge among all men of the sole deity of Jehovah (22)—a petition for the conversion of the Gentiles. The phrase in the last verse of the Song, θεὸς τῶν θεῶν, might be taken as an admission of the existence of other gods over whom Jehovah was supreme. But clearly this is not so intended, as may be proved from the use of the phrase in Deut. x. 17, Pss. xlix. I (LXX), cxxxvi. 2. Yet it is not unlikely that Nebuchadnezzar used the phrase in this acceptation in ii. 47. The other occasion, however, on which it is used in Daniel (xi. 36), allows it to be taken only in an orthodox sense; nor is any other likely in the mouth of Azarias, who resisted to the utmost the command to sin by idolatry. It is observable that Azarias omits the clause "in thy seed shall all nations of the earth be blessed" (Gen. xxii. 18, xxvi. 4) from his quotation of the patriarchal promise. This might arise from dislike to the nations, who had conquered Israel; but on the other hand, the gist of it is contained in his concluding petition in v. 22.

The objection that Ananias, Azarias, and Misael are invoked as saints (which probably caused the omission in 1789 of v. 66 (88) from the American P.B.) is sufficiently answered by pointing out that the Song is praise, not prayer; and that these three do not stand on a different footing in this respect from the other objects apostrophized. Moreover, a highly poetical composition of this kind is not to be too literally interpreted. As Liddon remarks in his *Elements of Religion* (Lond. 1892, p. 182), "The apostrophes of the Psalms and Benedicite are really acts of praise to God, of which his creatures furnish the occasion;" and Addison again (*Spect.* No. 327), "Invocations of this nature fill the mind with glorious ideas of God's works." v. 43 (65) is oddly applied by Archdeacon Frank, *Serm.* XLII. to Pentecost (Oxf. 1849, II. 254).

Belief is plainly shewn in an angelic ministry, sent down to help God's suffering servants, and endued with miraculous powers. The angel comes, too, after their humble confession and prayer for rescue (vv. 43-45), and before their song of praise. The very propriety however of this arrangement, from a theological point of view, induces Rothstein to deem the prayer a subsequent introduction, in order to supply the want of request for deliverance before praise for its accomplishment; and he thinks that the opening in the narrative for the insertion of the prayer (between vv. 23 and 46) was not, in the O´, very deftly effected (Kautzsch, I. 175, 181).

The natural and the supernatural, without any incongruity, are blended as being all under one control, all subserving the same great ends, as in the Hebrew Bible. But there is no increase of the miraculous element beyond that in chapter iii., in which this piece is inserted; and at a later age increase would have been highly probable. What essential difference is there to be found between the miracles of the Chaldee and of the Greek Daniel? Surely none.

A typical resemblance was discerned by St. Antony of Padua (*Moral Concordances*, ed. Neale, p. 123), between v. 26 (44) and the Annunciation, but this will be regarded by many minds as a very fanciful theological discovery, and one surely not in the purview of the composer of the passage.

CHRONOLOGY.

There is but little in the way of chronological indication in this addition; considerably less than in the other two, and what there is, is indirectly brought in.

A time after the Captivity is evidently pointed to in vv. 26, 32, 37, 38. Jerusalem was lying under a heavy visitation, the people delivered over to the enemy, almost denationalized, and deprived of the sacrificial worship to which they had been accustomed. Yet this position of affairs is spoken of as if it were not one of very long standing. (*Cf.* the use of νῦν in vv. 31, 33, 42, though in the last of these instances its use may not perhaps be temporal.)

It has been objected, quite unnecessarily, that v. 38 is inconsistent with v. 53, the one implying the destruction of the temple, the other recognizing its existence; v. 84, too, may be taken as supposing priests to be still capable of performing their offices. It is even possible that the corrections of Cod. A in v. 38 may have had behind them some idea of softening a discrepancy. This supposed lack of consistency has been taken as an indication of double authorship of the Prayer and the Song; and of course, if the Prayer were a later interpolation than the Song, even the appearance of contemporary inconsistency is avoided. But if we were to decline this hypothesis, and take Prayer and Song as from the same pen, there is still no real difficulty; for v. 38 is thinking of the earthly temple, v. 53 of the heavenly. Grotius (*Critici Sacri*), apparently accepting the statements of v. 38 as correct, writes: "Harum rerum penuria animos venture Evangelio præparabit."

Another chronological difficulty, that of "no prophet,"[25] in the same verse (38) has even been offered as a 'proof' of non-canonicity (Cloquet, *Articles*, p. 113). So T.H. Horne in Vol. IV. of his *Introduction*, quoted by A. Barnes on Daniel (I. 81), says that "v. 15 (38) contains a direct falsehood"; and in Vol. II. 937 of his *Introduction* (ed. 1852), he asserts that the author "slipped in the part he assumed." More just is his observation that "Theodotion does not appear to have marked the discrepancy." Ball, too, joins in the condemnation, by expressing an opinion that the writer had "lost his cue" (*Introd. to Song*, p. 308); and Reuss, "Hier verrät sich der Verfasser" (*O.T.*, Brunswick, 1894, VII. 166). It has been suggested (J.H. Blunt *in loc.*) that Ezekiel, who was both priest and prophet, had just finished his utterances, while Daniel, if he had commenced his, would, out of modesty, not reckon himself. The same commentator also attempts, still less successfully, to overcome the difficulty of "no prince." Probably, however, this merely means that no monarch was actually reigning, and that Jewish rulers were themselves ruled and their authority superseded, not that no member of the royal house or of the ruling classes was in existence. And this seems to fit in better with an early period of the Captivity than with a later age, when Simon Maccabeus is said to have had the title נָשִׂיא on his coins: and Mattathias is called ἄρχων in I Macc. ii. 17. Gesenius says in his *Thesaurus* under נשיא on the authority of F.P. Bayer (*de numis hebraeosamaritanis*, p. 171, append, p. xv.), that Simon's coins had the inscription שמצון נשיא ישראל[26]; but it is now doubted whether the coins formerly attributed to Simon are really of his time. (*Cf.* Bp. Wordsworth of Lincoln on I Macc. xv. 6.) Zöckler's idea (*Comm. in loc.*) that ἡγούμενος must be understood here as equivalent to "priest" is unsupported and needless. כֹּהֵן is never so translated by LXX.

[25] *Cf.* Ps. lxxiv. 9.

[26] See also H.J. Rose's Paper *On the Heb. coins called shekels*, Beds. Architect. Soc. Rep. I., p. 367, 1851.

Cornelius à Lap. (Paris, 1874), deals with the difficulty of "no prophet" in a different way. He writes, "Quia Dan. potius somniorum regiorum erat interpres, quam propheta populi; Ezech. autem propheta aberat agebatque in Chobar aliisque Chaldaeae locis, eratque is unus et captivus. Itaque 'non est,' *i.e.* vix nullus erat." Of "princeps et dux" he says nothing; but Peronne adds a note to say that Daniel was thinking of Judaea only. It is not unlikely that Hos. iii. 4 was in the mind of the writer of the Song, as being fulfilled in his days.

If, however, we assume a date for the whole piece considerably later than that of the canonical book, it is quite conceivable that the author may have made a backward transference of the circumstances of his own time to that of the earlier exile. For this is a species of error all traces of which even expert forgers find it difficult to remove.

It is generally assumed, and probably rightly, that v. 88 is intended as a contemporary utterance of the Three calling upon themselves; nevertheless it is quite intelligible as the expression of a later writer summoning them, with the rest of creation, to praise their Maker. And, assuming this verse to be contemporary with the rest, this latter idea would of course mark the hymn as not really issuing from the mouths of the Three.

Everything said and done in this piece takes place within one day, the day on which Nebuchadnezzar's subjects were ordered to worship the golden image. There is therefore much less scope than in Bel and the Dragon, or even

Susanna, for those who seek to discover chronological difficulties, because devotional compositions afford fewer openings than narrative matter for the raising of such questions.

CANONICITY.

Like Susanna, and Bel and the Dragon, the Song of the Three Children formed, so far as we know, part of the original LXX text of Daniel, having a connection with it closer even than theirs. For while they take their places at the beginning or the end, this one is incorporated into the narrative of chapter iii. as one connected whole. Prof. Robertson Smith does indeed write (*O.T. in Jewish Church*, 1895, p. 154), "these are perhaps later additions to the Greek version"; but this is only conjecture, and as such he puts it forward.

Until the correspondence of Origen with Africanus, the canonicity of these pieces does not seem to have been called in question by Christians who used Greek or Latin Bibles; nor do Greek-speaking Jews appear to have disputed the matter seriously. "Commonly quoted by Greek and Latin Fathers as parts of Daniel," says Westcott (Smith's *D.B.*, ed. 2, I. 713b). So Schürer (II. III. 185), "Julius Africanus alone among the older Fathers disputes the canonicity of these fragments." See also Bissell's admission on p. 448 of his *Apocrypha*. But Jerome seriously called their canonicity in question (*Præf. in Dan.*), although he included them in his translation, with a notice that they were not found in the Hebrew. Polychronius, Theodore of Mopsuestia's brother, refused to comment on this piece because it was not part of the original Daniel, nor in the Syriac, οὐ κεῖται ἐν τοῖς Ἑβραϊκοῖς ἢ ἐν τοῖς Συριακοῖς βιβλίοις. In this latter respect it keeps company with the Catholic Epistles in the earliest stage of the Syriac N.T. (Carr, *St. James*, p. XLVII). But it gained a place in the Peshitto (*D.C.B.* arts. *Polychronius & Polycarpus Chorepisc.*). Buhl (*Kanon und Text des A.T.*, 1891, p. 52) says that the Nestorians recognise "die apokryphischen Zusätze zum Daniel als kanonisch;" and the Malabar Christians regard this, with its two companions, "as part and parcel of the book of Daniel." (Letter to the writer from F. Givargese, Principal of Mar Dionysius' Seminary, Kottayam, 1902.) They formed part of the Sahidic, and probably other Egyptian versions of Daniel, which may be as early as century II.; as also of the Ethiopic and, seemingly, of the Old Latin (Swete, *Introd.* 96, 107, 110).

It seems very difficult to prove that the Alexandrian Jews who used the LXX did not regard this piece as canonically valid; though how they reconciled their canon with the Palestinian one is not clear. Their frequent communication with Palestinian Jews must have brought any considerable discrepancy to the notice of both sides. F.C. Movers (*Loci quidam Hist. can. V.T.*, Breslau, 1842, pp. 20, 22) solves the difficulty by imagining that this and the other Apocrypha were similarly regarded both in Palestine and Alexandria, "vix credibile est alios libros a Palestinensibus inter profanos repositos ab Alexandrinis codici sacro adscitos esse." Acts ii. 10 proves the presence of Egyptian Jews at Jerusalem for Pentecost, and vi. 9 that they had a synagogue there. This close connection must have brought their religious practices to one another's knowledge, and any differences, considered seriously important, could hardly have failed to raise disputes. Now Bleek (*Introd. to O.T.*, II. 303, Engl. transl, Lond. 1869), says "the additions to Esther and Daniel were certainly looked upon by the Hellenistic Jews in just the same light as the portions of the books which are in the Hebrew." And this seems to have been done almost without question, difficulty, or protest, although Alexandrian ideas must have been, brought under the notice of the religious authorities in Jerusalem. (*Cf.* Meyer's note on Acts vi. 9, and Jos. *cond. Ap.* I. 7, as to regular intercourse between Palestinian and Alexandrian Jews.)

Professor, now Bishop, Ryle (*Can. of Script*, p. 157) thinks that the amplification of Daniel, as of Esther, may have been tolerated because Daniel was not then deemed canonical. But we must remember that additional sections, though smaller in extent, appear in other books of the LXX, of whose canonicity there appears to have been no question, *e.g.* Job xlii. 17, Prov. xxiv. 22, I. Kings xvi. 28, this last being taken from chap, xxii., though still left there. It has also been suggested by Prof. Swete (*Introd.* p. 217) that the כתובים were probably attached to the canon by a looser bond at Alexandria than in Palestine. However this may be, certain it is that this addition was frequently quoted or referred to by early Christian writers as if part of Dan. iii., without qualification or sign of misgiving, as may be seen in the quotations given in the chapter on 'Early Christian Literature,' p. 76 *sqq.* Loisy's contention is a noticeable one (*A.T.* p. 236), "Presque tous les auteurs catholiques, anciens et modernes, qui ont emis des reserves touchant l'autorité des deutero-canoniques, ont regardés ces livres comme inspirés. Ils ne les croyaient pas bons pour établir le dogme; mais cela est parfaitement compatible avec l'inspiration, attendu qu'un livre peut-être inspiré sans être dogmatique, et que s'il n'est pas dogmatique par son contenu il ne saurait regler le dogme." But this contention savours somewhat of clever special pleading in order to evade the force of opposing evidence. Loisy, however, for a Roman Catholic, is a wonderfully frank and fair writer on these matters.

The explanation of the early mixture of non-canonical books with canonical, by reason of their having been kept as separate papyrus rolls in the same chest (Swete's *Introd.* p. 225), seems not an unlikely one in the case of independent works such as Judith or Wisdom. But it appears to lose its force in the case of additions such as these, or those to the book of Esther. For the Song of the Three, Susanna, and Bel and the Dragon are hardly likely to have had separate rolls assigned to them; least of all this first piece, which fits into the middle of the accepted narrative, and is scarcely intelligible without it. Something more therefore is wanting to explain the inclusion of those portions in the Greek Bible.

Bengel's explanation (*Gnomon on Matt.* xxiv. 15), that the apocryphal books in Latin Bibles were mixed with the canonical "pro argumenti affinitate," though distinguished at first by marks (afterwards omitted) in the index, however likely so far as it goes, fails to account for their admission on so slender a plea into Biblical MSS. at all.

If the additions are to be regarded with Streane (*Age of the Macc.* p. 161) as "specimens of fiction," this one, more strongly than the other two, shews the pre-existence of the canonical Daniel; but it is very hard to understand how 'fiction' of this kind could be introduced into the Bible with no general protest, and ultimately come to be treated as of Divine authority; and this position is defended, even in these critical days, by the greater number of Christians in the world.

When the Council of Trent made the canon of Scripture co-extensive with the Vulgate, this, with the other additions, was of course included in the decree. But in the Roman Church up to the present day attempts have not been wanting to minimize the force of this decision, which, if it removes some difficulties, certainly introduces others. Outside the Roman Church the position of these books, in common with the rest of the Apocrypha, remains, as always, more or less insecure.

A. Scholz, in condemning the principle that Christians are tied to the O.T. canon, rather amusingly supposes: "Wenn Jemand sich bei den Juden jetzt als Prophet geltend machen und ein Buch schreiben würdem so müsste es nach diesem Grundsatz von den Protestanten als kanonisch wohl anerkannt werden" (*Esther und Susanna*, Würzburg, 1892, p. 140). But such argument is mere polemic, which cannot be seriously taken into account in establishing the position of this or the other additions. Something is needed much deeper and more convincing in character.

EARLY CHRISTIAN LITERATURE AND ART.

LITERATURE.

In the N.T. *possible* references may be found in St. Matt. xi. 29 (ταπεινὸς τῇ καρδίᾳ) from v. 65 (87); II. Tim. i. 18 (εὑρεῖν ἔλεος) from v. 15 (38); [in Numb. xi. 15 only does the phrase elsewhere occur, but in another tense]; Heb. xii. 23 (πνεύματα δικαίων) from v. 64 (86).

Our 'apocryphon' is often referred to or quoted by early Fathers to a remarkable extent, considering the brevity of the piece and its merely episodic character in the main narrative. The following are specimens:

JUSTIN MARTYR (†167?), *Apol.* I. 46, Ἐν βαρβάριος δε Ἀβραὰμ καὶ Ἀνανίας καὶ Ἀζαρίας καὶ Μισαὴλ καὶ Ἠλίας καὶ ἄλλοιπολλοί. The names of the Three occur in this form and order in v. 88 of the Song only.

CLEM. ALEX. (†220) in his *Ecloga prophetica*, § I, quotes several verses with ἐν τῷ Δανιὴλ γέγραπται.

HIPPOLYTUS (†230) recognizes the Song of the Three in his comment on Daniel, *in loc.*, as well as in the Fragment preserved in the "Catena Patrum in Psalmos et Cantica" (*Ante-Nic. Christian Lib.* p. 484). In the former place he comments on the words καὶ διεχεῖτο ἡ φλόξ, and says that the Three ἐδροσίζοντο in reference to v. 50; in the latter, on the verse "O Ananias, Azarias," etc., he notes that everything is called to praise, ἵνα μὴ ὡς ἐλεύθερον αὐτεξούσιον νομισθῇ.

TERTULLIAN (†240) *de Orat.* § 15, says that they prayed, "in fornace Babylonii regis orantes." In § 29 he quotes vv. 26, 27.

ORIGEN (†254) *Comm. in Ep. ad Rom.* I. c. 10, II. c. 9, VII. c. 1; *Comm. in Matt.* XIII. c. 2 (naming the LXX); and in *de Oratione* XIII. XIV.

CYPRIAN (†258) *De lapsis* 31 and *De dom. orat.* 8, quotes this piece, in the latter case agreeing with Θ rather than Oʹ. Pseudo-Cypr. (some of whose writings Professor Swete, *Patristic Study*, 1902, p. 67, deems to be contemporary with Cyprian or nearly so) in *Oratio* II. 2 says "misisti angelum tuum cum roribus tuis," agreeing with Oʹ.

EUSEBIUS (†342), in his first *Fragm. on Daniel*, comments on iii. 49, ὡσεὶ πνεῦμα δρόυ διασυρίζον (Θ), and quotes Psalm xxviii. 7 as illustrative. (In Constantine's "To the Convention of Saints," given in the translation of Eusebius (Camb. 1683), much mention is made of Daniel in Babylon, but there is no clear indication of knowledge of the additions.)

ATHANASIUS (†373) quoted the Song in *Ep. Pasch.* x. 3; and in *Agst. Avians* II. 71 he employs the Song to "arraign the Arian irreligion" (Newman's translation).

EPHREM SYRUS (†378). His commentary on Daniel does not embrace the additions, but in his *Morning Hymn*, rendered by H. Burgess (Lond. 1853), we have "Sprinkle me with Thy dew, like the young men in the furnace."

CYRIL OF JERUSALEM (†386) quotes both the Prayer of Azarias (v. 29) and the Song (v. 54) in *Catech.* II. 18 and IX. 3 respectively, without hesitation (ed. Reischl, Munich, 1848).

AMBROSE (†397) *in Luc.* VII "Cantaverunt Hebræi cum vestigia eorum tactu flammæ rorantis humescerent."

HIERONYMUS GRÆCUS THEOLOGUS (cent. IV?) *de Trin.* treats the hymn, flames and dew in the furnace, μία κάμινος οὖσα, as an emblem of the Three in One.

SULPICIUS SEVERUS (†400?) *Hist. sacr.* II. § 5 shews knowledge of this Song by writing of the Three as "deambulantes in camino psalmum Deo dicere cernerentur."

CHRYSOSTOM (†407) *De incomprehensibili Dei natura* V. 7, οἱ τρεῖς παῖδες ἐν καμίνῳ διῆγον ... λέγουσιν, οὐκ ἔστιν ἡμῖν κ.τ.λ. *In Isaiam* VI. ἐπεὶ καὶ οἱ παῖδες οἱ τρεῖς τοῦτο αὐτὸ ἔλεγον σχεδὸν ἐν τῇ καμίνῳ ὄντες· οὐκ ἔστιν ἡμῖν ἀνοῖξαι τὸ τόμα. *Hom.* IV. *ad pop. Antioch.* (de statuis) τὰς ἱερὰς ἐκείνας ἀνπεμπον εὐχας. Also *De incarnatione* VI.

RUFINUS (†410) *adv. Hieron.* lib. II. upbraids Jerome for not reckoning the piece canonical.

JEROME (†420). In the *Comes* or Lectionary, the Song is made use of, but probably the Comes is not really Jerome's. (*See* art. *Lectionary, D.C.A.* 962a.)

THEODOERT (†457) in *Letter* CXLVI. quotes v. 63 amongst a string of canonical texts; and also deals with the whole in his *Commentary on Daniel*, as consolidated with chap. iii.

SEDULIUS (†460?). In his poem *De tribus pueris* there is nothing which goes beyond the canonical record; but, strangely enough, in his *Miraculorum recapitulatio proedictorum* there are the lines

".... flagrante camino
Servavit sub rore pios."

And equally in the prose version "rore sydereo puerorum membra proluit in camino." This shews a recognition of v. 50 (de la Bigne, *Bibliotheca Patrum*, ed. 4, 1624, pp. 660, 661, 914).

VERECUNDUS (†552) wrote a comment on some of the ecclesiastical canticles including the prayers of Azarias and Manasses (printed in *Spicilegium, Solesmense*, Vol. IV.).

It is manifest, therefore, that Early Christian writers regarded the Song as of much value and importance; were well acquainted with it, and often quoted it in much the same manner as the canonical books. Occasionally, however, a knowledge of it is not shewn where we should have expected it; and in some cases we know that those who quoted it denied, or doubted, its canonicity.

This Greek insertion in the book of Daniel has, on the whole, offered less scope for the exercise of artistic talent than the history of Susanna or even than that of Bel and the Dragon. The nature of its contents, which consists in the main of a prayer and a song, reasonably accounts for this paucity of illustration. It does not lend itself so readily as its two companions to pictorial treatment. Nevertheless a certain number of examples are not wanting.

Loisy in his *Canon of the O.T.* (1890, p. 95) remarks, "Dès avant le IVe siècle, on ornait les catacombes de peintures dont les sujets avaient été fournis par Tobie et les fragments de Daniel."

In a fresco from the cemetery of St. Hermes, the Three Children are represented, each over a separate stoke-hole (or what looks like one), with hands elevated as if in prayer or praise, most likely in reference to v. 1 (24), (*see D.C.A.* art. *Fresco*, p. 700a). Another picture of figures somewhat different, yet with outstretched hands, is given from Bottari in the same Dictionary under art. *Furnace*. There are sculptured representations of the Three on the high crosses at Moone Abbey, and at Kells (M. Stokes, *Early Christian Art in Ireland*, Lond. 1887, II. 22).

In the Utrecht Psalter, over the Song are depicted, as well as in other places, the sun and the moon, very appropriately (*D.C.A.* art. *Sun*), and in other illuminated Psalters, pictures of the Three in the furnace are not uncommon. Thus Brit. Mus. MS. Additional 11836 has an illumination of the furnace scene.

The under side of the wooden roof of Trinity College Chapel, Cambridge, was painted about 1870 with the series of natural objects mentioned in the Song proper, and with the words appertaining to each. A few extracts from *Benedicite* are on scrolls in a modern window on the south side of the chancel of St. James' Church, Bury St. Edmunds.

It is a little surprising that the series of objects named in this Song has not been more frequently chosen for decorative purposes on roofs, walls, or windows of ecclesiastical buildings, where a long series would be appropriate. Perhaps the length of the series, and the difficulty of making any but an arbitrary selection, has something to do with the rarity of its appearance.

A set of not very satisfactory wood-engravings by MacWhirter and others, one illustration to each verse, was published in a small book under the title of the *Song of the Three Children illustrated* (London, 1887)

The verse "O ye wells," etc., is said to be a frequent motto for the floral well-dressings at Tissington, in Derbyshire, and elsewhere, on Ascension Day; and a more appropriate one could hardly be found. But in general the Song of the

Three Children has not, for the reason given above, and doubtless others besides, proved a popular subject in art.

LITURGICAL USE.

GENERAL.

There is, strange to say, no record of the Song's employment in this way amongst the Jews. Statements sometimes made to the contrary in works on the P.B., *e.g.* by W.G. Humphry, F. Procter, E. Daniel, and J.M. Fuller (S.P.C.K. *Comm.* "Introd. to the Song"), "in the *later* Jewish Church," all appear to have originated in a misunderstanding of an ambiguous sentence in Wheatley's *Rational Illustration* (1875, p. 143). He says that it "was an ancient hymn in the Jewish Church." But this does not necessarily imply that it formed any part of Jewish services. Nor did Wheatley probably intend to assert that it did. In point of fact no evidence of such use is forthcoming, though it certainly would not have been surprising if the Song had been so used, at least among the Hellenistic Jews. For as Rothstein says in Kautzsch's Apocrypha, like Ps. cxxxvi. it is "offenbar antiphonisch aufzufassen" and "litaneiartig."

Notwithstanding the previous neglect, as it would seem, of this Song in Jewish worship, its use by Christians dates from an early period. So Bp. Gray (*O.T.*, p. 611) says, "It was sung in the service of the primitive Church;" and Ball, "the instinct of the Church, which early adopted the *Benedicite* for liturgical use, was right" (p. 307). Yet after it had come into high esteem with Christians its chances of Jewish acceptance would of course be largely diminished.

EARLY.

The liturgical use however was generally confined to the Song proper, commencing with v. 29, and not always extending to the whole even of that. In the Greek Church it is divided into two odes, said at Lauds on two different days, vv. 3-34 (A.V. verses) forming one, and the remainder of the Song the other (art. *Canticle D.G.A.*). In the Ambrosian rite the first part only of the Song is used as an invitatory before the Matin Psalms, under the title, somewhat confusing to us, of "Benedictus" (*D.G.A.* art. *Benedictus*).[27]

[27] In the *Bk. of private Prayer* (Lond. 1887, p. 32), approved by the Lower House of Canterbury Convocation, these six verses are employed as a separate canticle, under the title *Benedictus es*, probably suggested by the Ambrosian rite above mentioned. The same canticle had also appeared previously in *An Additional Order for Evening Prayer*, put forth by the same authority in 1873, for singing after the first lesson.

For some reason not easy to assign, the Song, whether divided or entire, has always been treated as a morning canticle, although there is nothing in its words to suggest any time of day as specially appropriate.

Rufinus, according to Dr. Salmon (*Speaker's Comm.* Introduction to Apocr. XXVIIb), speaks of the Song as "sung on Festivals in the Church of God." No reference is given to the passage quoted. But in Rufinus' *Apol. in Hieron.* II. 35 we find the words, "Omnis Ecclesia per orbem terrarum... quicunque Hymnum trium puerorum in Ecclesia Domini cecinerunt," etc. Whether this be the passage Dr. Salmon intends or not, it is at any rate sufficient to prove that the canticle was in use in and before Rufinus' time, who is believed to have died in the year 410.

Bishop Barry (*Teacher's P.B.*) notes that it was used at Lauds (τὸ ὄρθρον) in the East as well as in the West: and so Mr. Hotham in his art. *Canticle* in *D.C.A.* In his art. *Psalmody*, however, no mention is made of its Eastern use; but in the Western Church in the Gregorian and its derived rites, including the Roman and cognate Breviaries, he says, "Benedictiones sive canticum trium puerorum" comes in Sunday Lauds, and likewise in the Benedictine Psalter.

In the Ambrosian Psalter, while the first part "Benedictus es" is said daily at Matins as stated above, the usual *Benedicite* is said at Lauds on Sundays. In the Mozarabic Psalter an abridgment of both parts is said at Lauds, but not "in feriis." "Benedictus es" also comes on weekdays at Prime. In the Mozarabic Missal *Benedicite* occurs in the service for the first Sunday in Lent. In the use arranged by Cæsarius of Aries (†542) for the Gallican Church *Benedicite* was sung at Sunday Lauds.

Duchesne says (*Christian Worship*, Eng. tr. S.P.C.K. 1903, p. 195), "In the Gallican Mass between the Apostolic and the Evangelic lections the Hymn of the Three Children was sung. It was known also by the name of the Benediction (*Benedicite*) because in it the word 'Benedicite' is continually repeated." In a note he adds, "The Luxeuil Lectionary, however, prescribes for the Nativity, *Daniel cum Benedictione, i.e.*, the Hymn of the Three Children before the Apostolic Lection. It is true that in the Mass of *Clausum Paschale* it places it after this lection."

The fourth council of Toledo in 633, condemns the omission of the Song at Mass, threatens with excommunication those who in Spain or Gaul (or Gallicia, margin) persist in leaving it out, and styles it "Hymnum quoque trium puerorum in quo universa coeli terræque creatura dominum collaudat et quem ecclesia catholica per totum orbem diffusa celebrat" (Mansi, *Concil.*, Florence, 1764, X. 623).

In the Roman Missal at the end of the Canon, the last Rubric is "Discedens ab Altari, pro gratiarum actione dicit Antiphonam Trium Puerorum cum reliquis, ut habetur in principio Missalis;" where is given as an antiphon before it these words, "Trium puerorum cantemus hymnum quem cantabant sancti in camino ignis, benedicentes Dominum."

Possibly there is a reference to this Eucharistic use in Bishop Wordsworth's Michaelmas Hymn, No. CII. in his *Holy Year*, 1864.

Angelic voices we shall hear
  Joined in our jubilee,
In this thy Church and echoing
  Our Benedicite.

Angelic faces we shall see
  Angelic songs o'erspread
Above thy holy Altar, Lord,
  And Thou, the Living Bread.

In the Saram Breviary (and in Cardinal Quignon's) *Benedicite* is a canticle at Lauds on Sundays only. It is to be said without "Glory"; "dicatur sine Gloria Patri per totum annum quandocunque dicitur" (Procter, p. 188); but a doxology is provided in the Roman Breviary, "Benedicamus Patrem et Filium cum Sancto Spiritu," etc., and 'Amen' is directed not to be said at the end. This doxology is said to have been added by Pope Damasus I., who also transposed v. 56 to stand as the finale of the Song (*see* James M'Swiney, *Psalms and Canticles*, Lond. 1901, p. 643). This R.C. writer calls the use of the canticle on Sundays "a thanksgiving for the resurrection of the Crucified, the earnest of the glories wherewith nature is to be invested at His second coming." But this sounds like an *ex post facto* reason for its appropriateness.

Benedicite appears, at any rate sometimes, to have been said subsequently to *Te Deum* after the election of an Abbot (*see* Jocelin of Brakelond's *Chronicle*, Sir E. Clarke's ed., 1903, p. 38). It also appears in the *Cantica* after the Psalter, between *Te Deum* and *Benedictus*, in the Scottish *Breviarium Bothanum*, which is thought to be of about 15th century (Lond. 1900).

Thus it is evident that the use of this hymn became general at an early period, and so continued, having never receded in Christian esteem as a valued factor in public worship.

Besides the use of the Song, or part of it, as a canticle, verses or small portions often occur in liturgies; *e.g.*, vv. 28-30 are borrowed in an Ἐκφώνησις before the offertory prayers in the Liturgy of St. James; at the censing of the Gospel in that of St. Mark; in a Byzantine Liturgy of the ninth century in the second prayer of the faithful; in that of St. Chrysostom immediately before the lections in the Mass of the Catechumens; and v. 19 in the Ἐπίκλησις in that of the Coptic Jacobites (Brightman's *Liturgies*, I. Oxf. 1896). In the Leonine *Sacramentary*, in a Preface, Mense Junio, IIII. 1. 13, ad Fontem, the last words of the Song appear to be cited "plena sunt omnia saccula misericordia tua" (Dr. Feltoe's ed., Camb. 1896, p. 31). The verse "Benedicite omnes angeli" occurs in a "Communio" for Michaelmas in the Rosslyn Missal; "Benedictus es Domine patrum nostrorum" occurs in the Mass of the Holy Trinity in the Westminster Missal as a "gradale," also in a Mass "pro sponsis", and other places (Hen. Bradshaw Soc., Lond. 1899, p. 70, 1897, p. 1239). v. 34 (56) occurs in the Sarum Compline after the Creed, as also in the Roman.

In the Greek Euchologion a great part of the Song is embodied, with other Scripture odes, in what is styled "the Canon at Great Matins in the All Night Vigil" (*Euchology*, translated by G.V. Shann, Kidderminster, 1891, p. 34).

LATER ENGLISH USE.

Burbidge (*Liturgies and Offices of the Church*, 1885, p. 268), gives a number of instances of the use of *Benedicite* in foreign service books, and says, "In other churches *Benedicite* has been held in higher esteem than amongst ourselves." Esteem for it has never been entirely lacking, however, as its prominence in the P.B. shews.

In a Prymer of circ. 1400, as given by Maskell (*Mon. rit.* 1882, Vol. III. p. 21), *Benedicite* occurs in Matins, beginning "Alle werkis of the Lord, bless ye to the Lord: herie ye and overhize ye him in all time." On the same page, note 49, he gives a quotation from *Gemma animae*, II. 53, "canticum trium puerorum est festivius et ideo in omnibus festis dicitur." Also in his *Append, to Prymer*, p. 243, another version is given, from Bodl. Douce MS. 275, fol. 9b: "Alle werkes of the Lord, bless ye the Lord: praise and overheie ye him in to the worldes." There was an authorized translation into Welsh early in the 14th century, according to H. Zimmer (*Urtext und Uebersetz*, Leipzig, 1897, p. 172), together with *Magnificat, Benedictus*, and several Psalms, evidently for liturgical purposes.

In the P.B. of 1549 the use of the *Benedicite* as a substitute for the *Te Deum* was confined to Lent "all the which time" its recital was obligatory. It has been suggested by W.G. Wyon (*Letter to "Guardian,"* May 14, 1902) that mediæval devotion read into it an allegoric meaning of deliverance from temptations and dangers of this naughty world, and this made the Song suitable for Lent. He also suggests that the 'Oratio' of the Roman Missal in the 'Gratiarum actio' after Mass, which contains it, shews us its suitability for penitential seasons indirectly, "Deus qui tribus," etc. No doubt hope of deliverance from fierce spiritual perils may be in Lent a proper frame of mind; but this attempt to prove the *Benedicites* special appropriateness to that season is more ingenious than satisfying. It is strained and far-fetched. Compare what is said above (p. 88), where M'Swiney is cited as shewing in similar style its special appropriateness to Sunday. The tone of the canticle is unmistakeably joyful, and the 1549 rubric disappeared in 1552, leaving *Benedicite* as a simple alternative to the *Te Deum*, at any time according to the taste of the officiant. And so it still remains, though often preferred to the *Te Dewm* during Lent. Septuagesima and Trinity XXI. are, on account of their first lessons, fitting Sundays for its use; nor is it by any means unsuitable for a harvest festival. An entirely different kind of reason for its Lenten suitability is provided by H.P. Cornish (*Notes on P.B.*, Evans, Redditch, n.d., p. 17). Lent, he says, is the time "when all nature begins to wake from its Lenten sleep": hence its appropriateness in spring. It is questionable, however, whether mediæval liturgical authorities paid much attention to the natural seasons of the year; and the variety of 'reasons' proves the difficulty of discovering a really conclusive one. The idea that the *Benedicite* is consonant with Lenten feelings is singularly out of accord with the opinion expressed as to its character as being 'festivius' in the *Gemma animae*, given above, p. 90. Indeed it can hardly be disputed that its tone is joyful. But though its special aptness for a fasting-time is not easy to make out clearly, few unprejudiced people will dissent from the opinion of Freeman as to its scope when he writes, that "though wanting in the grand structure of the *Te Deum*, in point of range it is in no way inferior" (*Divine Service*, Lond. 1855, I. 356).

In the scheme for the revision of the Prayer-Book in William III.'s reign it was actually arranged to expunge *Benedicite*, and to substitute Ps. cxlviii. It would have been extruded in good company however, as *Magnificat* and *Nunc Dimittis* were to be replaced by psalms in a similar way. Happily the deplorable proposals of 1689 came to nothing. But strange to say, previously to this, in the Laudian Scottish Prayer-Book, Psalm xxiii. had been substituted for *Benedicite*. In England, however, in 1662, the Church, taught by the persecution of the Commonwealth, declined "to appoint some psalm or scripture hymn instead of the apocryphal *Benedicite*", as demanded by the Puritans at the Savoy Conference (Procter, *P.B.*, 1872, p. 119).

At a rather earlier period, Dean Boys of Canterbury, in his quaint *Prayer-Book Notes* (1615?) says: "I finde this hymne less martyred than the rest, and therefore dismisse it, as Christ did the woman (John viii.), 'Where be thine accusers? Hath no man condemned thee? No more doe I; goe thy way.'"

At least three English metrical renderings of *Benedicite* exist, one of the 18th and two of the 19th century, by J. Merrick, J.S. Blackie, and Richard Wilton respectively. The first of these writers, who expands freely, concludes with a stanza designed to put the Song unmistakeably into the mouths of the Three:

Let us, who now impassive stand,
Plac'd by the Tyrant's stern Command
  Amid the fiery Blaze,

(While thus we triumph in the Flame)
Rise, and our Maker's Love proclaim
  In hymns of endless praise.

The objection that in using this hymn we pray to angels and heavens, to ice and snow, etc., shews how hard it is to find reasonable cause of complaint against its use. (*See* p. 62).

The whole canticle was however actually omitted in the P.B. printed at Oxford in 1796, an edition notorious for the liberties taken with the book in many ways (A.J. Stephens' *P.B.*, Lond. 1849).[28] The last verse, "O Ananias," etc., which was omitted in the United States' P.B. is, as well as the above, dealt with under 'Theology,' p. 64.

[28] Its use declined in the 18th century as is shewn by P. Barclay (*Letter to People of Scotland on Comm. Pr.*, Lond. 1713, p. 36), who says, "Benedicite is very good; but because it is seldom or never used, I don't insist upon it." P. Waldo (*Commentary on Liturgy*, 1775, p. 98), also deplores its disuse. And even in the 19th century C. Chaplin (*Benedicite*, 1879, p. 11) says, "In a few churches it seems to be banished from the service altogether."

In an *Altar Service Manual*, ed. 1837, which was very popular in the middle of the 19th century, by S. Isaacson, certain extracts from the *Benedicite*, with presumably original additions, are formed into what is called "the canticle" in an "Evening Liturgy for use after Holy Communion." The five added verses, in rather unrhythmical English, are modelled in imitation of the Song, *e.g.* "O ye who have partaken of the Holy Communion, bless ye the Lord: praise Him and magnify Him for ever."

The Song of the Three Children is, with other canticles, frequently found in appendices to both Greek and Latin Psalters. And on this account it is included sometimes in commentaries on the Psalter, as in that of de Muis (†644), Louvain, 1770, beginning with v. 51, "tunc hi tres quasi ex uno ore laudabant," etc. It stands in this book between Hezekiah's and Jonah's prayers. In the mediæval Psalters, *Benedicite* may constantly be found, though its place in the series of canticles varies considerably.

Many of the LXX MSS. too contain these canticles, or some of them, repeated from their regular places in the text, such as Alexandrinus and the Veronese and Turin Psalters; of these the first has vv. 26 to 45 and 52 to 58, as two separate canticles between the Prayer of Manasses and Magnificat; the second, vv. 52 to 90 after Magnificat as its last canticle; and the third has vv. 26 to 45, 52 to 56, and 57 to 90 as three separate canticles between the P. of M. and Benedictus. In each case, it will be observed, the narrative portion is naturally excluded.

In the first and third of these MSS., A. and T., it may here be noted that there is a non-biblical Morning Hymn, Ὕμνος ἑωθινός, a kind of Eastern "Gloria in excelsis," which contains an apparent extract from vv. 29, 30 (52), or v. 3 (26) of our Apocryphon, in line 34 of the hymn. Very nearly the same words occur in Tobias' song (Tob. viii. 5), which curiously enough (in common with the song of Deborah), is not included in these canticles. Doubtless it was not in ecclesiastical use; but the reason why the Christian Church abstained from availing herself of it for choral purposes is not evident; any more than why the Jewish Church abstained from the use of *Benedicite*.

Although the employment of *Benedicite* in the services of the Church is interesting, as shewing the value set upon, and the use made of, this canticle, it reflects little or no light on its origin, or indeed on any of the heads under which it has been previously discussed.

"EXAMPLE OF LIFE AND INSTRUCTION OF MANNERS."

The conduct of Azarias and its results shew us the *value of Prayer* made by those under persecution. He led the way, and his comrades joined him.

Azarias is not so taken up with the wrongs of himself and his fellows as to forget the wrongs which his own nation had done; therefore his prayer commences with a *humble Confession*. Then he relies on the great promises of the past (vv. 12, 13). It may be thought that *Humility* is also shewn in the Song by the Three putting their own names in the last place of the series. But another cause may have contributed to the choice of this order; for, so far as animal life is concerned, the Song follows the order of Gen. i., bringing in human beings last, not as being least important, but as forming the crown of creation.

Although Nebuchadnezzar is severely spoken of in v. 9, A.V. (and in iv. 27 of the canonical book 'sins and iniquities' are attributed to Nebuchadnezzar), there is great *Self-restraint* shewn in wishing for retribution (vv. 20, 21); and indeed it is asked that he and his servitors may be brought to the knowledge of God (v. 22).

The pleasure of *Thanksgiving and Praise* on delivery are exemplified by the Three in the production of the Song itself. As soon as ever their prayer was answered, before they emerged from the furnace, they united their voices in thanking God with a glow of fervid faith, recognizing in Him the universal Lord and Benefactor.

They sang in harmonious accord their song of praise at once (v. 28). Though staunchly refusing to worship in a wrong way, they were very ready to do so in a right, and lost no time in proving it, publicly and before all creation. As de Muis (†1644) says in his *Comm. in Psalmos* (Louvain, 1770, II. 705), "Ut calamitatibus tanquam igne probatur; fidelis animus non modo non deficiat sed etiam animata inanimaque omnia ad Dei laudes provocet." Eager to honour God, they join in unreserved devotion.

Their *Reliance upon God* is obviously great. To Him they turn in their martyrdom with prayer and praise; to Him they address themselves with the heart and voice of sure conviction. He is their unfailing resource.

A *Love of Nature*, as created by the same hand as ourselves, is very apparent in this canticle; there is a thorough fellow-feeling with natural objects, as derived from, and responding to, the same Almighty source. This love of nature appears in Holy Scripture most strongly, as here, in the poetical books, and hardly anywhere does it take a deeper tone than in this canticle.

PART III
THE HISTORY OF SUSANNA

כְּשׁוֹשַׁנָּה בֵּין הַחוֹחִים
(שיר ב׳ ב׳)

THE HISTORY OF SUSANNA.

ANALYSIS. (Θ)

vv.

1-4. Susanna—her husband, family, and house.

5,6. Two newly-appointed Elders resort thither for official purposes.

7-14. How they yielded to the 'lust of the eye,' and laid their plot.

15-21. How they attempted to carry it out.

22-26. Susanna's soliloquy and cry.

27-41. The Elders' false accusation in private and in public, resulting in her condemnation to death.

42-44. Her prayer.

45-49. The inspiration of Daniel to clear her.

50-59. He re-opens the case, and proves the Elders to be false.

60-62. The death-penalty is transferred to them, and Susanna is delivered,

63, 64. Whose family thank God; while Daniel's reputation is established.

N.B.—It is not clear why the 'heading' or 'contents' in the A.V. *begins* with v. 16. *Cf.* the heading of Bel and the Dragon for a similar ignoring of the early verses, as also that of I. Macc. i.

TITLE AND POSITION.

TITLE.

This is in general simply Σουσάννα, as in the true LXX.

In Cod. A (Θ) it is designated at the end ὅρασις α', our chap. i. being ὅρασις β', and so on. It is therefore included in the number of the visions.[29] Ὅρασις also occurs in the title of Holmes and Parsons' cursive 235.

[29] It is stated in Dr. Swete's *Introd.* (1902, p. 260) that Susanna is excluded from the visions, Dan. i. 1 commencing the first of them. But this is not borne out by the 'apparatus criticus' to his Greek text, where i. 1 in A and Q begins ὅρασις β', and ὅρασις α' is the subscription of Susanna in A.

In the Syriac of Heraclius (=W₂ of Ball, pp. 323a, 330a) it is entitled "The Book of the child Daniel," or "The Book of little Daniel" (Churton, 3896). This last title also seems applied to Bel and the Dragon in a Nestorian list mentioned by Churton (on the same page), and in Ebed Jesu's list of Hippolytus' works (*D.G.B.* art. *Hippolytus*, p. 104a), When applied to Bel and the Dragon, however, 'little' must refer to the size of the book, and not, as is usually understood when it heads Susanna, to Daniel's youthful age. To this Bar Hebræus (†1286), in his Scholia on Susanna, expressly attributes it (ed. A. Heppner, Berlin, 1888, p. 18). He also remarks that neither Syriac version is equal to the Greek.

"The Judgments of Daniel," Διακρίσεις Δανιήλ, is a good title given by Arnald, by Churton (p. 390), and by Westcott (Smith's *D.B.* art. *Additions to Daniel*, ed. 1, 3966, ed. 2, 713b), none of whom specify any source or authority for it, Arnald alone giving the Greek. It may be traced back, however, through Sabatier to Flaminius Nobilius, who writes, "In multis [vetustis libris] inscribitur Daniel, in quibusdam Susanna, in aliquo διάκρισις Δανιήλ, Judicium Daniel" (Append, to Bp. Walton's *Polyglott*, Lond. 1657, p. 191). He gives no information as to what this 'certain' copy at the end of his descending climax might be in which he had found this title; nor does it quite agree with the plural form in which Arnald gives it, presumably with regard to the double sentence passed by Daniel. Holmes and Parsons give no such reading, and no one now seems able to identify the 'liber' intended by Flaminius. Delitzsch (*di Hab. Vita*, etc., Lips. 1842, p. *25n*) says that "Unus Cod. qui ex coenobiis montis Athos advectus est" gives the title περὶ τῆς Σωσάννης.

As this piece describes one episode only in Susanna's life, "the History of Susanna" in both A.V. and R.V. is not a good title. 'History' and 'story,' however, were not so clearly differentiated in English formerly as they are now. Possibly this title was taken from Jerome, who speaks of "Susannæ historiam" twice in his Preface to Daniel. It is given also in Syr. W₁. In Article VI., and in the "Names and Order of the Books" in A.V., it takes the form, "Story of Susanna."

The name שׁוֹשַׁנָּה is so eminently fitted to the subject of the story as to suggest its intentional choice; and, so far, would tell in favour of the allegoric, and against the historic, nature of the piece[30]. Or even supposing the piece to be historic, the name may have been assumed in order to avoid identification of the heroine. The word occurs in its masculine form, שׁוֹשַׁן, in I. Chron. ii. 31, 34, 35; and in its feminine form in II. Chron. iv. 5, Cant. ii. 1, 2 (here in a phrase most readily lending itself as a motto for the tale), and Hos. xiv. 5. The place Shushan, too, is thought to have been named from the abundance of lilies which grew there. This name, derived from the plant world, is paralleled by that of Habakkuk in the companion story of Bel and the Dragon, according to Marti on Hab. i. 1 (*Hand-Commentar,* Tübingen, 1904).

[30] The name is used of an actual woman in St. Luke viii. 3.

POSITION.

In Cod. Chisianus, and in the Vulgate, Susanna forms chap. xiii. of Daniel. So also in the Syro-Hexaplar version (Ball, p. 330b). Cajetanus Bugati (*Syriac Daniel,* Milan, 1788, p. 163), endeavours to explain this (against Michaelis) by supposing Susanna to have been removed from its original place at the beginning of the book.

In Codd. A, B, Q, Susanna stands at the beginning, before our chap. i. of Daniel. This is its position also in the Old Latin, and in the Arabic versions (Ball, p. 330b). Rothstein in Kautzsch (p. 172) thinks that this was not its original place, but the one in which Theodotion fixed it, or perhaps that which found favour when Theodotion's translation was substituted for LXX. And this position appears to be contemplated by the A.V. and R.V. titles, "set apart from the beginning of," etc. Driver, however, thinks (*Comm. on Dan.,* p. xviii.) that the chap. xiii. position (before Bel and the Dragon) was perhaps its original place. "The fact that it contains an anecdote of Daniel's youth might readily have led to its subsequent transference to the beginning of the book."

St. Hippolytus, a writer subsequent to Theodotion, evidently regards it as the commencement of the book (Schürer, *H.J.P.* ii. iii., 185). Flaminius Nobilius in his "Notae," as given in the Appendix to Bryan Walton's *Polyglott,* writes, "Hæc Susannas historia in omnibus vetustis libris est principium Danielis, quemadmodum etiam apud S. Athan. in Synopsi." This Synopsis is now considered to be of post-Athanasian date; and the position which its writer gives to Susanna in § 41 does not look quite consistent with that he gives afterwards in § 74 (*see* 'Canonicity,' p. 157).

Although in the Vulgate this moveable fragment forms Daniel xiii., Jerome, notwithstanding, in his Preface names these additions in the order, Susanna, The Three, Bel and the Dragon; yet in the immediately following "capitula Danihelis," it stands as in the text after chap. xii. This clearly points to some uncertainty as to its proper place.

The statements made by E.L. Curtis at the end of art. *Daniel* in Hastings' *B.D.,* that this and Bel and the Dragon are separate books in the LXX, have question marks justly affixed to them. In the Jacobite Syriac, Susanna is joined with Judith, Ruth, and Esther, as a "Female Book" (*Urtext und Uebersetz.* p. 230). Gwynn says (D.C.B. art. *Thecla,* IV. 895b), that in "Syriac O.T.'s these are usually placed together and classed as the four books of the 'Book of Women.'"

Yet another position is suggested by J. Fürst (quoted in Bissell, p. 444), who thinks its proper place is after Dan. i. 20. This is a very plausible conjecture, but evidence to support it is at present wanting. A slight confirmation of it however is afforded by the *Byzantine Guide to Painting* (*see* 'Art,' p. 171); and by the position given by Sulpicius Severus to his epitome of the story (*see* 'Christian Literature,' p. 167). E. Philippe (Vigouroux, *Dict.* II. 1267a) attempts to account for its removal from, or want of position in, the Massoretic Daniel, "parce qu'elle est infamante pour les juges d'Israel," obviously adopting Origen's reason (*see* 'Canonicity,' p. 157) which is not a very satisfactory one.

All things considered, the position of Susanna in the A.V. as a detached piece, along with Bel and the Dragon, is as suitable as any which have been suggested. For its original place cannot now, from the information in our hands, be determined with absolute certainty.

DATE AND PLACE OF WRITING.

DATE.

Susanna is deemed by J.M. Fuller (*Speaker's Comm., Introd. to Dan.*, 221a) to be probably the oldest of the three additions. This opinion is however by no means universally accepted.

If a Semitic original really existed, it no doubt preceded the Greek texts. R.C. opinion (*e.g.* Dereser, quoted by Bissell, p. 444), as that of all who regard the booklet as canonical, treats it as part of Daniel, and therefore whatever date is assigned to that book is made to apply to this also. Professor A.A. Bevan (*Comm. on Dan.*, Camb. 1892, p. 45) thinks that this piece and Bel and the Dragon "appear to have been circulated independently before they were incorporated with the book of Daniel." C.J. Ball ascribes the origin of the piece to the struggles between the Pharisees and the Sadducees, B.C. 94-89 (p. 330a). But to attribute it thus to the outcome of these quarrels, brings the original down to a later date than is at all probable, in view of its incorporation with the LXX.[31] Nor does the bitterness of those disputes seem stamped with sufficient strength upon the document itself to compel us to see in them its period of origin.

[31] Kothstein (Kautzsch i., 176) gives the first quarter of the last century B.C. as the latest possible date for the LXX version of Daniel. Exceedingly little time therefore would be allowed, on Ball's theory, for

the original publication, the translation, and the incorporation into the Alexandrian canon, of this Susanna-book.

J.T. Marshall (Hastings' *D.B.* IV., 631-2) conjectures that the latter part of the story arose out of Simon ben Shetach's efforts, about 100 B.C., to get the law as to witnesses in criminal cases altered. This view is perhaps a trifle more probable than Ball's.

As to the true LXX text, Bissell (p. 444) rather inclines to deem it to have been from the first a part of the LXX. So Pusey, quoted by Churton (p. 389), says that it is "admitted to have been contemporary with the LXX version;" and W. Selwyn (*D.B.* III., p. 1210a) thinks that this, with the other additions, was "early incorporated with the LXX." Rothstein in Kautzsch, very hesitatingly and with much caution, suggests (I., p. 178) the second century before Christ.

On the other hand, A. Kamphausen (*Encyclop. Bibl.* I. 1013) writes," When [Daniel] first began to be translated by the Egyptian Jews into Greek, the legends of Susanna and Bel and the Dragon, which may very well have had an independent circulation, had certainly not as yet been taken up into it.... We cannot tell at what date it was that these apocryphal additions (which are contained in all MSS. that have reached us), were taken up into the Greek and Syriac Daniel." How he knows so "certainly" that they were not in it at the period named, he does not explain; and before this positive statement can be unreservedly accepted strong proof is wanted.

As to Theodotion's version, there is no reason to suppose that the portion consisting of Susanna differs in date from the rest of the book. It may probably be assigned to the latter half of the second century A.D. Behrmann, in Nowack's *Hand Kommentar*, p. xxx. says, "um 150."

Most writers on this subject, such as Westcott, Streane, and Marshall, as well as some of those previously mentioned, markedly avoid any approach to definite dates as to the original, or as to the LXX Greek. And justly so; for the evidence in our hands does not, unfortunately, admit of anything closer than a "period" being safely fixed. The materials we have are not sufficiently precise for closer approximation with any decree of security. Rothstein (Kautzsch, I., p. 178) very wisely says, "Natürlich lasst sich mit irgend welcher Sicherheit über diese Frage nichts ausmachen." With this, until further evidence be forthcoming, it is well to agree.

PLACE.

Of Original. As to the place of origin nearly every writer on Susanna is silent except Scholz, who (p. 147) favours a non-Alexandrian birthplace, giving a preference to the land of the Captivity. And if we assume, as he does, a

Semitic original, Babylonia is no doubt its probable birthplace, or, failing that, Palestine.

It might appear, if the trees named could be botanically identified with a reasonable degree of certainty, that a valuable sign would thus be given of the place of origin. But inasmuch as Joacim's park or garden would be a likely place for the cultivation of exotics, perhaps no safe theory could be built upon the identification of the trees, unless they were shewn to be such as would not live in the climate of the country suggested.

There is no trace of Alexandrian philosophy or speculation, nor of commercial interests, some of which generally betray themselves in writings of Alexandrian origin. And the same may be said of the Song of the Three, and Bel and the Dragon. But in such short pieces it is not wise to build much on the absence of these traces.

Of LXX Greek. That this was made at Alexandria admits of little doubt. From the similarity of style, too, it would appear that the translator (or editor) was identical with the translator of the canonical Daniel. This is the opinion of Rothstein (in Kautzsch, I. 178). Schürer (*H.J.P.* II. III.), who denies the existence of a Semitic original, classes this (with the other additions) not in his 'Palestinian-Jewish,' but in his 'Graeco-Jewish' section.

The mention of Sidon in v. 56 (where Θ has Canaan) may perhaps suggest a writer in the original, whatever language he may have used, who was connected with the north of Palestine. But it is quite as probable that the writer (or translator) had some idea of Gen. x. 15 in his mind, "Canaan begat Sidon his firstborn." After him, according to Josephus (*Ant.* I. VI. 2), the city was named: Σιδώνιος ὃς καὶ πόλιν ἐπώνυμον ἔκτισεν ἐν τῇ Φοινίκῃ, Σιδὼν δ᾽ ὑφ᾽ Ἑλλήνων καλεῖται. It is worth noticing that in St. Matt. xi. 21 our Lord speaks of the city more favourably.

Of Theodotion's Greek. Of the 'provenance' of the Greek version bearing Theodotion's name very little is known. But Ephesus may be suggested as not altogether improbable with regard to what little we know of Theodotion's life. If we take the Revelation of St. John, too, as having been written at Ephesus, this will accord well with the use made of Theodotion's version of Daniel in that book. Or if Theodotion made use, in whole or in part, of some previous version, as seems certain, this fact would not at all militate against St. John at Ephesus having also made use of the same earlier version. And it is quite possible that this version may have been of Alexandrian origin, although worked up by Theodotion elsewhere.

Whatever the place of origin may have been, it is very remarkable that a version by one who was either a Jew or a heretic Christian should have been preferred to the LXX of Daniel and the Additions so as practically to supersede it. Prof. J.J. Blunt describes Theodotion as one who "attempts to wrest the Hebrew from the cause of the Gospel" (*Christian Church*, p. 129). This was indicated by Irenæus, III. xxiii. 1. If, however, the previous version used by him was due to a pre-Christian Jew, this may have smoothed the way for its acceptance among Christians. For Jews B.C. and Jews A.D. were regarded by the Church, as was natural, in very different lights, and their writings likewise.

AUTHORSHIP.

Like some other of the apocryphal books, this is a traditional story of great popularity. It is not necessary to suppose that its author's name has been lost from the title, as it may always have been anonymous. The nature of its contents would not be unlikely to give offence to the Sanhedrin, and therefore a motive for anonymity is not far to seek.

Bishop Gray (*Introd. to O.T.* p. 613) seems, as he often does, to hit the mark, as nearly as we can tell, when he deems it to be "by some Jew who invented the history, or collected its particulars from traditionary relations in praise of Daniel." This observation is little more than paraphrased by J.H. Blunt, when he writes (*in loc.*) "probably inserted into LXX from some ancient Jewish authority." The variations of text certainly suggest an oral tradition, perhaps even more strongly than in Bel and the Dragon.

Bissell says that Susanna "contains nothing which might not have come from the pen of a Hellenist" (p. 445); and Westcott sees in this and other additions "the hand of an Alexandrian writer" (Smith's *D.B.* ed. 2 I. 714a), but thinks it not unlikely that he worked up earlier traditions. Certainly v. 22 seems to shew that the author of the Greek of Θ was evidently acquainted with the LXX of II. Sam. xxiv. 14. "Wer die Susanna (in Walton's *Polygl.* 4) nach Theodot. frei übersetzt hat," says Nestle, "wissen wir nicht" (*Urtext und übersetz.* 236).

It is noteworthy that Josephus shews no acquaintance with this or the other additions, though he makes some use of other uncanonical legends of Daniel (*Jud. Ant.* X., 10, 1; 11, 6 and 7). Schürer in Hauck's *Encylop.* (I. 639), thinks Susanna and Bel and the Dragon may well originally have had independent existences. If so, this might help to explain Josephus' disregard of them.

It is a reasonable inference from v. 57, that the author was a Jew in the strictest sense, and not from one of the ten tribes. Yet it should not escape notice that in v. 48 "Israel" is apparently used for the entire people, including all the tribes.[32] The invidious contrast between the Israelitish and Jewish women is omitted in what Dr. Salmon calls, "the second Syriac recension" of Susanna, termed erroneously at one time "the Harklensian" (*Speaker's Comm.*,

p. xlvi.). The contrast in v. 56 between Israel and Canaan is made into a stinging reproach, but is hardly to be understood literally as to the Elder's family descent.

[32] If not, as Bissell in his note elegantly puts it, "it would be a bungling lapsus pennæ."

J. Kennedy in *Daniel from a Christian standpoint* (p. 55), says of this and the other Additions that there is "no means of determining when, where, or by whom written." He adds (p. 56), "those who conceived and wrote the additions were both intellectually and spiritually incapable of appreciating the book [of Daniel] and its contents," and he concludes that they "belong to different ages and to entirely different conditions of thought." This estimate is a much too severe one, and very different from the opinion formed by some other equally qualified judges. The fear lest a favourable opinion of the quality of these pieces should lend any countenance to the Tridentine decree as to the Apocrypha, or seem to weaken the Protestant position with regard to them, appears to have operated, consciously or unconsciously, in shaping the views on this subject expressed by such writers. Probably acting under similar sentiments Ludovicus Cappellus, †1658 (quoted by Ball, 325a), calls the author "a trifler" (nugator), and styles his production "fabula ineptissima."

Jerome, in the Prologue to his *Commentary on Daniel*, says that Eusebius and Apollinarius replied to Porphyry's objection to these additions that "Susannæ Belisque ac Draconis fabulas non contineri in Hebraico, sed partem esse prophetæ Abacuc filii Jesu de tribu Levi;" and apparently acquiesces in this statement. As there appears to be no other authority for attributing Susanna to Habakkuk, it is a question whether the LXX title to Bel and the Dragon was not applied to Susanna also "per incuriam." A. Scholz escapes the difficulty of Habakkuk both here and in Bel and the Dragon by regarding it as a merely symbolic title, which he renders by "Kämpfe" on very slender grounds (*Esther und Susanna*, Würzburg, 1892, p. 138; and *Judith und Bel und der Drache*, 1896, p. 204).

It must not be forgotten, however, that the authorship of Daniel is of course suggested by most of those who defend the canonicity of the book. Origen in his Epistle to Africanus maintains the solidarity of the piece with the book of Daniel. And it should be remembered, as a point of some strength, that Julius Africanus' correspondence with Origen at the beginning of century III., is the first record we have of any dispute as to its genuineness.

Professor Rothstein, in Kautzsch (i. 172) gives very decidedly a contrary opinion, stating that Susanna and Bel and the Dragon, "haben mit dem Danielbuche nur insofern zu thun, als in ihnen Daniel eine Rolle spielt." But it is hard to offer conclusive proof that Susanna and Bel and the Dragon differ greatly in character from the independent historical "scenes" of which the first six chapters of Daniel consist; each, in nearly all respects, being intelligible when standing alone. It is hard also to shew that their incorporation, and constant acceptance, with the LXX was a deplorable mistake. And this difficulty is enhanced when we see that, so far as is known, all the Greek and Latin speaking Christians before Julius Africanus, and most of them after, fell unquestionably into what, if Rothstein and those who think with him are right, must be deemed a grave error. But even if it could be proved that these pieces were by the author of Daniel, the recent questions as to who that writer may have been, still further complicate the at present insoluble problem of the authorship of Susanna.

FOR WHOM AND WITH WHAT OBJECT WRITTEN.

FOR WHOM.

That this story was originally prepared for the use of Jews there can be no doubt. Probably it was designed for readers and admirers of Daniel, who would be glad of this example of the prophet's insight. Certainly it was for those who loved to dwell on the interventions of God for His people, and especially on a recent manifestation of His particular care for oppressed individuals. Possibly also the case of those may have been regarded who were dissatisfied with the current methods of administering justice and conducting trials. J.W. Etheridge (*Jerusalem and Tiberias*, 1856, p. 109) deems it to be an example of Haggadah in common with its two companion pieces, "histories coloured with fable," as he styles them—a sort of legendary appendix to carry on the interest of readers of the canonical text.

But since the Christian era this writing has been employed by Christians far more than by Jews. Perhaps its ready acceptance by the former may have diminished the chance of popularity amongst the Israelites of later times. They would look upon it with more suspicion, though it was clearly connected with the literature of their race. And obviously this enlarged acceptance among Christians was beyond the aim of the tale's author.

WITH WHAT OBJECT WRITTEN.

The holding up an example of purity, maintained under circumstances of great distress, is the leading object which Christians have seen in this piece. It is probable, however, that other aims as well as this entered into the mind of the writer.

A dissatisfaction with the method of conducting trials such as Susanna's is clearly manifested. A Pharisaic, or at least an anti-Sadducean, tendency has been observed, particularly in the latter part of the story. Then the utility of investigating small particulars is demonstrated, and the necessity of a rigorous punishment of false witnesses, points on which the Pharisees insisted, according to Ball (329b, 330a), who quotes Simon ben Shetach as saying from the Mishnah (*Pirke Avoth*, I. 9) את הצדים הוי מרבה לחקור. Bissell (p. 447) also thinks that "to reform the method of conducting legal processes" was an object of the author. And certainly the story does teach the need for a close investigation of testimony.

The author shews up the unscrupulousness and injustice practised even in the leading circles of the Jewish community; and in so doing he manifests throughout a good knowledge of the workings of the human heart. Marshall (in Hastings' *D.B.*) assumes "that we have here an ethical mythus" (631b).[33] But to imagine that the story had no other origin than this is, to say the least, unproved, and, as many think, unproveable.

[33] This may be merely an echo of Reuss, who reckons Susanna "in die Reihe der moralischen Märchen" (*O.T.* 1894, VII. 159).

Another object may have been to extol Daniel and his judicial acumen. There is a resemblance in this respect to the tone of several chapters of the Book of Daniel, *e.g.*, ii. and iv. His penetration and his prophetic gifts as a young man are set forth. Indeed the last two verses of the O´ version almost make the praise of youthful piety the moral of the book. But this, edifying as it may be, is scarcely to be taken as the chief object of the composition; and Θ substitutes another conclusion as to the gratitude of Susanna's family and the growth of Daniel's reputation.

Still, apart from the question of historic value, many worthy objects may have lain within the purview of the composer; and to shew that righteous youths are better than unrighteous elders may very well have been one of these. To prove that even men of riper years are not unerring in judgment may well also, as G. Jahn (quoted by Ball in *Speaker's Comm.* 325a) points out, have been a subsidiary aim.

The kind of judicial acumen displayed strikes one, too, as being very similar to that of the young Solomon in his judgment on the two women (I. Kings iii.); but the story here is not an imitation of that. It is a wholly distinct instance of the same class, a most popular one for narration in Eastern countries.

Another object in writing this history (and certainly the most useful object from a Christian point of view) is to give an example of the maintenance of purity and right, even at the risk of losing both life and reputation.

It may be questioned, however, whether the idea of depressing the estimation of elders, or of raising that of Susanna and of Daniel, was uppermost in the writer's mind. Almost equal prominence is given to each of these ideas. The latter, perhaps, would throw over the piece a somewhat less attractive character than the former. But there is that in the cast of the composition which suggests that its object may have been quite as much to raise disgust at the elders' crime as to raise admiration at Susanna's purity; in fact that the whiteness of her character was designed as a foil to make more prominent the blackness of her oppressors. On this account Jer. xxix. 23 might perhaps be taken as a verse which gave his cue to the writer. But these are points on which opinions will inevitably vary according to the impression made on different minds by a matter so nearly balanced.

This, the only one of our three booklets in which women appear, presents them in a very favourable light. Beyond the imputation suggested against those of Israel at the beginning of v. 57, it contains nothing but what is creditable to the female sex. The present Archbishop of Armagh's poem, "The Voyage to Babylon," thus prettily depicts Susanna's purity:

".... garden bed of balm,
In one whereof old Chelcias' daughter
Went to walk down beside the water,
The lily both in heart and name,
Whose white leaf hath no blot of shame."

Abp. ALEXANDER'S Poems (Lond. 1900).

INTEGRITY AND STATE OF THE TEXT.

In Θ we appear to have the story presented to us without material interpolation; but there are omissions of some not very important matters contained in the LXX text. A. Scholz accounts for variations by supposing changes in the Hebrew original between the times of the two translations. Of Θ he says, "Θ ist nichts als Uebersetzer; er setzt de suo kein wort bei" (p. 142)—an exaggerated statement.

The true LXX version was long supposed to be lost; but a cursive MS. of it (9th or 10th century) was found in Cardinal Chigi's library at Some, and was first printed in 1772. From its owner's name it has received the title of Cod. Chisianus, and is now numbered 87.

It is almost certain that Θ must have had the O′ text before him, since the coincidences of diction, though not so continuous as in the Song of the Three, are still far too numerous to be accidental. Bissell (p. 443) says of all the three pieces, "Θ simply recast the version of LXX." This dictum, however true of the Three, must not be quite literally taken of Susanna, as he does introduce some fresh matter, particularly at the opening and the close. Prof.

Rothstein in Kautzsch (pp. 176-7) thinks that the two Greek versions are two independent forms of the same story, based on some common narrative material; but when the obvious idea presents itself that this last was an Hebraic original, he speaks with much guardedness (p. 178), lest he should commit himself to this view.

Θ's recension is rather more polished in language, less elaborate in some of its details.[34] Fritzsche, quoted in Kautzsch (pp. 176-7), says that "he worked over the LXX text, expanded the narrative, rounded it off, and gave it a greater air of probability." Westcott's opinion to a similar effect, however (Smith's *D.B.* ed. 2 I. 714a), is called in question by Professor Salmon (*Speaker's Comm.* XLVI.a), who thinks that there is quite as much to be said for the opposite views, and this opinion is reasonable.

[34] *See* J.M. Fuller in S.P.C.K. *Comm. Introd. to Sus.*

In the LXX text there is surely something wanting at the true beginning at v. 5, which, as it stands, is awkwardly abrupt. Both Bissell (and Brüll, quoted by him, p. 457) approve of the idea that the beginning was suppressed because of its containing damaging reflections on the elders. Then the present opening (vv. 1-5) was borrowed from Θ, and is marked in both Cod. Chis. and Syro-Hex. as not part of the original work, but a foreign exordium. Rothstein (p. 184, note) thinks that in place of the present borrowed commencement there stood a short introductory remark on the two judging elders. Though lacking proof, this conjecture is well within the bounds of possibility. Yet in the Syro-Hexaplar text the first five verses are obelised, indicating, according to Bugati (p. 163), that they are omitted in Θ, but present in O´.

There are in the LXX extra clauses, which are not in Θ, scattered throughout the book; three verses between 14 and 15, one at the end, and considerable enlargements of vv. 45, 52; also curious substitutions, such as that in v. 39, where in the LXX the imaginary young man escaped because he was disguised; in Theodotion, because he was stronger than the Elders. These alternative reasons are of course not of necessity incompatible.

The Syriac W_2 (=Harklensian) contains many further particulars inserted here and there, such as the Elders' names (Amid and Abid)[35], v. 5, Daniel's age of twelve years, and some words in praise of him, v. 64. But most of these added clauses may not unfairly be regarded as 'paddings,' put in by way of embellishment. Those in v. 41 (ninth hour), v. 45 (twelve years of age), v. 64 (increase in favour) have a Christian look, the last two being suggestive of a knowledge of St. Luke's Gospel (*cf.* 'Style,' p. 140). Also the continuation of v. 43 in Lagarde's second Syriac version has rather a Christian air, "appear for me and send a Redeemer from before thee," etc. (Hastings' *D.B.* art. *Sus.* p. 631b).

[35] These names, however, do not agree with the Jewish identification of them, as the Ahab and Zedekiah of Jer. xxix. 21, which Origen reports in his *Ep. ad Afric. (Speaker's Comm.* 325b).

An attempt has been made to account for the numerous, but not generally very important, variations in different texts and versions by supposing the story to have been a favourite oral narrative, long continuing in a fluid state. This is far from improbable.

The Vulgate, which follows Θ closely, appends the first verse of Bel and the Dragon as the conclusion of this story. If this was done in order to avoid chronological difficulty there, it was at the expense of introducing it here, and that, to all appearance, very meaninglessly.

The chief uncial MS. authorities for Θ's text are A,B,Q, and from v. 51 onward, Γ. A often agrees with Q, as in vv. 19, 24, and elsewhere, in substituting πρεσβύτεροι (O′'s word) for πρεσβῦται; in vv. 10, 11, etc., in substituting ἀπαγγέλλω for ἀναγγέλλω; and in v. 46, καθαρός for ἀθῷος. In the canonical part of Daniel the substitution of ἀπαγγέλλω for ἀναγγέλλω mostly holds good also so far as A is concerned (ii. 9, 16).[36] In v. 36, A has a transposition of a clause, and in v. 39 another of its changes of prepositions in composition, not easily accounted for. Q (alone) has such changes in vv. 4, 32, 38. The above are all changes from B. Γ often agrees with A and Q, or both, but has nothing of importance independently.

[36] So in N.T., St. Mark v. 19.

The genitive Σουσαννάς (instead of ης) occurs occasionally in all the above MSS. (vv. 27, 28, 62; also in LXX, v. 30). *cf.* Μάρθας in St. John xi. I.

Two cursive MSS. (234 Moscow, S. Synod; 235 Rome, Vat.) consist of Susanna only; but whether they are perfect, or only fragments, is not clear. Holmes and Parsons give no particulars. On the whole, the text of either version is fairly trustworthy, the average of variations being not at all above that in the canonical Daniel.

LANGUAGE AND STYLE.

LANGUAGE.

As with the Three, so here, the question at once arises, Is the Greek of the LXX more probably the original language or a translation? The acceptance of a Semitic original seems on the whole to be more in the ascendant than formerly; but still, the greater part of those who have expressed an opinion on the subject incline to Greek as the language chosen by the author.

The Hebraic style is somewhat less strongly marked than in the other two fragments, nor has an Aramaic text of this one yet been discovered. Still, the Greek can be rendered into Hebrew rather more easily than most Hellenistic Greek. The Greek of the "rest of" Esther differs much more in style and tone from that of the canonical book to which it is attached than does the Greek of Susanna from that of the canonical Daniel; and, so far as this fact goes, it points to a closer linguistic connection in this case than in the other (*see* Streane, *Age of Macc.* p. 160; Bissell, p. 203). Delitzsch (*op. cit.* pp. 31, 101) says that "particulæ quædam citantur a Nachmanide" (entitled מגלת שׁשׁן) as well as of Wisdom. The citations of the latter book are discredited by Farrar (*Speaker's Comm.* p. 411) however, and probably those of the former are in a similar position.

The early place of verbs in the sentences is here also, as in the other pieces, to some extent noticeable as conforming to the theory of a Semitic original. If the etymology of the name דניאל is supposed to be drawn from his 'judgments' in this story, such an original is probably involved in the supposition (*cf.* 'Title,' p. 104). The Hexaplaric marks mentioned by Bugati (*op. cit.* 156), as occurring at the beginning of Cod. Chisianus (A, Σ, Θ), are strongly suggestive of translation (*cf.* Song, 'Language,' p. 49).

The controversy which was started by Africanus with Origen (and resumed by Porphyry[37] with Eusebius of Cæsarea, and by Rufinus with Jerome) as to the famous play upon the names of the trees (vv. 54-60) is still unsettled. Some see in the paronomasiæ conclusive proof of the originality of the Greek; others still contend with Origen that they are no certain evidence as to determination of language. But few will think the analogous case which he (Origen) gives from Gen. ii. 23 a very convincing one (*D.C.B.* art. *Heb. Learning*, p. 858b). Still we must remember that the Hebrew language was fond of paronomasiæ, and that Daniel employs the figure in the canonical book (v. 25-28). In other O.T. instances of its use it is, however, difficult to to see that the LXX made any attempt to reproduce the word-play, *e.g.* Isai. v. 7, Mic. i. 10; nor does either Greek version in Dan. v. 25-28.[38] But ἄνεσις and ἄφεσις in I. Esd. iv. 62 looks like a word-play in what may not be original Greek; though a Semitic original of that section of I. Esd. (iii. 1 to v. 6) is by no means proved.

[37] *Adv. Christ.*, Bk. XII.

[38] For similar instances of word-play see accounts of Melito's pseudo-Clavis, *D.C.B.* iii. 897b, and Muratorian Fragment, line 67.

It has been shewn, however, in the case before us, how an adequate play might be produced in Aramaic, as also in English (Hastings' *D.B.* art. *Sus.*). A. Scholz, too, in his Commentary attempts this, with only moderate success, in Hebrew[39]; and Delitzsch (*op. cit.* 102) gives some Aramaic possibilities of it from Plessner. As the precise punishments named were not carried out, this passage in the original, whatever it may have been, was clearly constructed with a view to introduce their names.

[39] Jerome in his *Prol. gal.* shews how it might be done in Latin; and in the Vulgate some attempt is made to reproduce it in vv. 54, 55 ('schinus, scindit'). Luther tried after rhymes in German, 'Linden,' 'finden,' 'Eiche,' 'zeichnen.' In the French version of Martin no play is attempted; but in the Arabic, according to Delitzsch (*op. cit.* 102), an easy one is produced.

It is interesting to compare and contrast the account of the Woman taken in Adultery (St. John viii.) with that of Susanna, the one truly, the other falsely, accused. There are, as might be expected, some verbal parallels, but not sufficient to prove that the N.T. writer was influenced by the History of Susanna, nor to give us material assistance in deciding its original language (*cf.* III. 'Language,' p. 49). Notwithstanding the general inclination towards Greek, this must at present be left in doubt, and a verdict of 'non liquet' given.

In the following observations on specific points in the language, instances telling in both directions have been included:

v. 3 O´, Θ. The use of κατά after διδάσκω, instead of a double accusative, suggests a translation of למד followed by a ב or מן, with either of which it is sometimes constructed.

v. 5 O´, Θ. If Aramaic be the original language, ἐδόκουν may well represent צְבָא, as in IV. 14, V. 23 and elsewhere.

v. 6 O´, Θ. Scholz deems κρίσεις and κρινόμενοι to be based on a confusion between משפטים and נשפטים.

vv. 7, 15, 19, 28 Θ. καὶ ἐγένετο is suggestive of ויהי.

vv. 8, 14, 56 O´, Θ. The use of ἐπιθυμία in a bad sense, and of ἐπιθυμέω in a perfectly innocent one in v. 15 Θ, seems careless, and may point to translation from an original, where different roots were used, *e.g.* אהב,חמד,אוה. *Cf.* LXX of Deut. v. 21 (18) for a rendering of two different Hebrew roots by the same word, ἐπιθυμέω, though in that case they are both employed in a bad sense.

v. 15 Θ. καθὼς ἐχθὲς καὶ τρίτης ἡμέρς looks like כִּתְמוֹל שִׁלְשֹׁם, as in Gen. xxxi. 5 and II. Kings xiii. 5. "Wörtlich hebräisch," as Reuss notes *in loc.* If Aramaic were the original, it might be וּמְדָקְדָמוֹהִי כְּמֵאֶתְמָלִי.

v. 17 Θ. σμήγμασα, "exprimere voluit Heb. בורית," but תמרוק (Esth. ii. 3, 9, 12) seems quite as likely as this suggestion of Grotius. Both roots are Aramaic as well as Hebrew.

vv. 11, 30, 39, 63 Θ. An instance similar to that given above (vv. 8, 14, 56) is the use of συγγενέσθδι in a bad sense in vv. 11, 39, and συγενεῖς innocently in vv. 30, 63.

v. 19 O´. συνθέμενοι = זמן either in Aramaic or Hebrew, as in ii. 9, while ἐξεβιάζοντο = כבש, as in Esth. vii. 8.

v. 22 Θ. Συενά μοι πάντοθεν occurs also in David's choice, II. Sam. xxiv. 14 (closer than I. Chron. xxi. 13). The certainty of its being a translation in the one place increases the probability of its being so in the other, suggesting a common original, unless we suppose a Greek author borrowing a Septuagintal phrase.

v. 23 O´, Θ. On the other hand, the participial clause in this verse in both versions seems un-Hebraic in form; as also the phrase ὁ τῶν κρυπτῶν γνώστης in v. 42 Θ, which is not very like a translation from the Hebrew. There is a certain resemblance to Dan. ii. 28, 29 (O´, Θ), ὁ ἀποκαλύπτων μυστήρια, however; but the latter contemplates God as revealing mysteries to others, the former as knowing secrets Himself.

v. 26 Θ. Scholz' idea that πλαγίας = קרי (as in Lev. xxvi. 21, etc.) would suit either Aramaic or Hebrew.

v. 27 Θ. Adduced as Hebraism in Winer's *G.T. Grammar* (*E.T.* 1870, p. 214); apparently, but not very clearly, on the strength of the phrase πώποτε οὐκ ἐρρέθη.

v. 36 Θ. The genitive absolute is Greek in character, but does not occur in O´.

v. 44 Θ. Εἰσήκουσεν... τῆς φωνῆς. A Hebraism, as in Gen. xxi. 17, and often.

v. 53 O´, Θ. The quotation is exact in both versions from the LXX of Lev. xxiii. 7. This fact may be thought to tell slightly in favour of a Greek original. In the canonical Dan. ix. 13 there is a reference, without precise quotation, to Moses' law, so that this mention is not out of character. The phraseology of the verse in Θ has a distinctly Hebraistic look, much more so than in O´.

v. 55 O´, Θ. ψυχήν, κεφαλήν = נֶפֶשׁ Isai. xliii. 4.

v. 56 O´. The epithet μικρά, as applied to the ἐπιθυμήα of the Elder, is inappropriate, and suggests an error of translation. Now טמאה is rendered by μικρά in Josh. xxii. 19[40], and this word would yield a very good sense in a Semitic original here, supposed to lie in the background.

[40] Μιαρά for μικρά would yield good sense, but evidence for such a reading is absent.

v. 57 O', Θ. If an animus against Israel, as Judah's inferior, is really shewn here it would point to a Babylonian, and therefore Semitic, original, inasmuch as the enmity between Israel and Judah does not appear to have been so strong at Alexandria. The use of 'Israel,' however, in v. 48 seems to include all in the first instance, and to be employed of Susanna specially in the second, who was presumably of Judah. The Syro-Hexaplar omits what was most likely deemed an invidious reflection. The reference to Hos. iv. 15 in the *Speaker's Comm.* (note) does not seem apposite as to its mention of Israel and Judah in the LXX; only in the Hebrew.

The phrase τὴν νόσον ὑμῶν comes in strangely, as Θ, by omitting it, apparently thought. It is suggestive of a translation, perhaps of חֳלִי, which seems to be used of moral disease in Hos. v. 13, and is there rendered by νόσος.

v. 59 O', Θ. Why ὑμᾶς? In LXX it comes in very awkwardly, where σε would naturally be expected.

Scholz, not improbably, suggests that μένει (Θ) and ἕστηκεν (O') have been caused by reading קוה and קום respectively, renderings which are actually found of those words elsewhere in the LXX, *e.g.* Isai. v. 2 and Dan. ii. 31. That confusion sometimes occurred between ה and the final ם is known.

v. 61 Θ. Τῷπλησίον, though referring to Susanna, may be a translation of רֵעַ, a word apparently regarded by Gesenius as epicene; so in Gen. xxiii. 3, 4, 8 τὸν νεκρὸν is the rendering of מֵת, meaning Sarah's corpse, "sine sexus discrimine" (Ges.). But πλησίον may be used here of 'neighbour' collectively without exclusive reference to Susanna.

v. 62 O'. Φάραγξ, a frequent translation of גְיְא or נַחַל. As it does not appear that there are any natural ravines in Babylon, this might refer to a deep moat outside the wall.

v. 64 (62) O'. Scholz says, "Εἰς ist sclavische Uebersetzung von ל das der Hervorhebung des Objektes dienen soll." This is probable, though 'sclavische' seems an unnecessary epithet.

STYLE.

The style is that of a clearly-told narrative, with little of a strained or rhetorical character about it; indeed there is less of this than in much of the canonical Daniel. Ideas are well expressed and the story well proportioned. There is nothing superfluous; everything bears on the main theme. Nor is it unnatural that Daniel is made to use a play on words out of the Elders' own mouths in order to render his sentence of condemnation more strikingly emphatic.

There is high literary skill in the simple yet effective way of narration. The story is a practical example of the saying, "Ars est celare artem," a fact which will be best appreciated by any who will try to tell the tale as well in their own words.[41] Holtzmann calls it, "besonders von der Kunst vielfach gefeierte Novelle" (Schenkel's *Bibel Lex.* 1875).

[41]

"And that which all faire workes doth most aggrace,
The art which all that wrought appeared in no place."

SPENSER, Faery Queene, II. XII. 58.

The lack of spontaneity and original freshness sometimes charged[42] against the apocryphal books is by no means conspicuous here, nor, though perhaps less decisively, in the next addition, Bel and the Dragon. The exciting interview between Daniel and the Elders is so drawn as to arouse much interest. By the first incident the whole current of Susanna's life is abruptly changed, and her destiny is made to hang in the balance for some time in a natural, but very effective, manner. The writer has a deep knowledge of the principles and actions of human feeling, and a thorough grasp of the art, by no means so easy as it looks, of telling a short story in a very engaging style. Plot, surprise, struggle, unfolding of character, and much else which is regarded as contributing to excellence in such a composition, we find here.

In the so-called Harklensian (W₂ of Salmon = Churton's Syr.[42]) various details are added, such as the judgment chair brought out, which Daniel refuses, standing up to judge; Susanna's chains (27, 50); her tears (33, 42); and her condemnation to death at the ninth hour (41). These are obviously designed to heighten, by the introduction of more detailed particulars, the effect of the narrative. The tale is so interesting and so true to nature that its popularity is easily explained. That it became a favourite story, in an age not given to prudery, for reading and for oral repetition, is not surprising. Like all such, it was subject to changes of form and gradual accretions. Oral repetition, as well as non-canonicity amongst the Jews will, to a considerable extent, account for the divergences between the LXX and Theodotion's recensions. The latter, in Reuss' opinion (VI. 412), "ist reicher an Einzelnheiten und auch besser stilisiert." With this view, in the main, most will feel themselves in accord.

[42] *I. Macc.*, Fairweather and Black, Camb. 1897, p. 14; Streane, *Age of Macc.*, Lond. 1898, pp. 247, 248.

RELIGIOUS AND SOCIAL STATE.

RELIGIOUS.

An unexceptionable O.T. moral standard on the part of the writer is maintained throughout, so that no 'difficulties' arise on this score. There is not a suggestion of any worship beside that of the Lord; no idolatry is even hinted at. The Captivity had done its work in that respect. Nor is there any symptom of the later developments of rabbinism; not even in their inception.[43] It requires a very sharp eye to find here so much as the germs of error in faith.

[43] Curiously enough the canonical Daniel has not escaped this accusation, for G. Jahn (Leips. 1904, p. 64) says of vi. 28, "Der König wie ein jüdischen Rabbiner predigt."

The Law of Moses is acted upon; taught by parents to children (v. 3); regarded as the great authority (v. 62). The institution of Elders is in full force, as contemplated in Jer. xix. 1 and xxvi. 17. I. Kings xx. 7 and xxi. 8, 11 shew that this body had been continued among the separated tribes, and so naturally carried with them to their new home. The appearance of corruption among officials in high places, who ought to have been most free from it, is quite in accord with the religious history of mankind in general, and of Israel in particular. Such references as the above to Jeremiah, and that in v. 5 to Jer. xxix. 23, are paralleled by a reference in the canonical Dan. ix. 2 to Jer. xxxv. 12.

When Daniel's plan was efficacious for revealing the Elders' guilt, the just decision was approved; the right is thoroughly commended and the wrong condemned. The heart of the people rings sound; their instincts at the trials are in favour of justice. Morality is supported by popular sympathy, which has been purified and elevated by the discipline of exile.

In v. 57 some prejudice is suggested as existing in the writer's mind against the women of Israel as being less chaste than those of Judah. Possibly he was of the latter tribe himself (*see* 'Language' on v. 57, p. 137). The reproach to the second Elder of Canaanitish descent is in keeping with Ezek. xvi. 3, where it is hurled against Jerusalem and her abominations.

It is objected in Hastings' *D.B.* (IV. 631b) that "Daniel loudly condemns both culprits before he adduces any proof of their guilt." But surely this was justified by the prophetic office and the spirit within him, which endowed him with an abnormal insight into the true state of affairs. Personally he was assured, from the outset, of their guilt, but secured public proof to satisfy the people. This objection is rather poor ground on which to assail the historic character of the piece. In fine, a religious tone, befitting the time intended, is consistently maintained throughout.

SOCIAL.

Incidentally a pleasing picture of home life is outlined, before the Elders tried to corrupt it.

Some of the Jews were apparently living in wealth and comfort during the Captivity; but the end of v. 4 shews that Joacim's estate was pre-eminent, not a sample of the general condition of the exiles. If not royal (as Jul. Afric. in his letter to Origen hints, and Origen doubts in his reply, § 14), it was evidently of an upper class; and a kind of tribunal was held at his house. The state of life here depicted agrees with Jeremiah's advice in xxix. 5; and with II. Esd. iii. 2, if that too could be applied to the captives.

The King of Babylon was content with the subjugation and deportation of the Jews, allowing them considerable liberty when he got them into Babylonia. In this connection Ps. cv. 46 naturally occurs to the mind. The captives evidently had alleviations granted them in Babylon by their conquerors, witness Evil-Merodach's kindness to Jehoiachin, II. Kings xxv. 28. There is, however, no indication even of the beginnings of that trade and commerce which was so characteristic of much of the dispersion in later years.

Great freedom to regulate their own affairs is shewn, including, to all appearance, the power of inflicting the death-penalty, v. 62. This last power has been objected to as unhistoric. But J.J. Blunt[44] illustrates the possibility of this, by citing Origen's letter to Africanus to shew that the Jews under the Romans enjoyed a similar power in his day. Origen defends the correctness of v. 62 by adducing this as a similar instance in his own knowledge. Blunt treats the matter as a kind of "undesigned coincidence," rendering credible the death penalties spoken of in Acts ix. 1, xxii. 4, xxiv. 6.[45] So Edersheim (D.C.B. art. *Philo*, p. 365b), "The rule of the Jewish community in Alexandria had been committed by Augustus to a council of Elders." This is also stated in the Jewish Encyclopædia (New York and Lond., *Alexandria* I., 362a): "Philo distinctly states that at the time of Augustus the 'gerusia' assumed the position of the 'genarch.' This is the word he uses for 'ethnarch,' *Contra Flaccum*, § 10. Origen to Africanus, § 14, writes of this privilege as having been granted by 'Cæsar' without specifying which Cæsar, and though he does not name Alexandria, his words ἴσμεν οἱ πεπειραμένοι probably imply that place." These references do not of course prove that the Jews in Babylonia had the like privileges, but they shew, as Origen saw, a parallel case. Perhaps those who are in favour of the Alexandrian origin of Susanna might use this to shew that the writer had transferred to Babylonia the circumstances of his own day; but his own day would almost certainly be before the time of Augustus.

[44] *Right use of Early Fathers*, Lond., 1857, p. 649.

[45] See Wordsworth, *Gk. Test.*, note *in loc.*

There is no mention of any government except the Jews' internal administration; but then the native population of Babylon (unless perchance it be in the shape of the servants) does not enter into the story. The legal working at Babylon of this little "imperium in imperio" had plainly an unsatisfactory side, although Susanna's rights were vindicated by another power against injustice and oppression. Still, it may not be fair to condemn the whole system on the strength of this single instance.

The main drift of the tale indicates the existence of much corruption[46] in the presbytery; yet the heart of the exiled people in general had a healthy tone; witness the sorrowful sympathy with Susanna (v. 33), and the delight at justice being ultimately done (vv. 60, 63).

[46] Quintus Curtius (v. 1) gives a terrible account, in connection with Alexander's capture of this city, of Babylonian debauchery, which must have been of long standing when it had attained the pitch he indicates.

The Elders grossly abused Joacim's hospitality. Seemingly they had plenty of time to waste, and worse. It is noteworthy that two 'judges' were chosen, annually, it would seem, from the 'elders of the people.' This last phrase occurs in Numb. xi. 16, and is frequent in the N.T., but not with ἐκ as here.

The modest veiling of Susanna in *v. 32*, more distinctly expressed (ἦν γὰρ κατακαλυμμένη) in Θ than in O′, reminds one of Rebekah's veiling in Gen. xxiv. 65, and is quite in accordance with the custom of the country. So are the "oil and washing balls" of *v. 17* (A.V. and R.V.); this last term is peculiar, and is used apparently for soap.[47] It is so employed in Gerard's *Herbal*, ed. 1633, p. 1526, where he says, "of this gum [storax] there are made sundry excellent perfumes... and sweet washing balls." The 'sawing' or 'cutting asunder' of *v. 35* was a Babylonian punishment, as is shewn in ii. 5 and iii. 29 of the canonical book.

[47] "Soap making is the chief industry of modern Palestine" (Hastings' *D.B.* art. *Soap*).

The death penalty for adultery (*vv. 43, 45*) is in agreement with Lev. xx. 10, Deut. xxii. 22, and Ezek. xvi. 38, though not with the laxity of later times (*see* art. *Adultery*, Smith's *D.B.*; *Marriage*, Hastings' *D.B.*). The Syriac W_2 interpolation after *v. 41* seems to regard precipitation as equivalent to stoning.

In the O´ of v. 62 both this punishment and that of fire are meted out to the Elders as retributive justice. Reuss' note on the trial is amusing, "die Richter sich als Dummköpfe erwissen und Susanna vollständig den ihrigen verloren hatte."

But we are disposed on the whole to agree with J.M. Fuller (S.P.C.K. *Comm.*, *Introd. to Sus.*) when he writes, "The facts underlying the story are in themselves probable," rather more than with Churton (p. 392), who deems the narrative to be "probably apocryphal, without strict regard to historical facts."

THEOLOGY.

This 'History' does not appear to have been written with a view of supporting any erroneous or debateable points in theology.

God is represented as being in heaven, as One on whom the heart relies (v. 35); as eternal, a knower of secrets, of entire foreknowledge (v. 42); One to be appealed to by His servants in danger (v. 43), efficaciously answering humble requests. The value of ejaculatory prayer to Him in sudden peril is shewn (v. 44).

God had not so entirely cast off His people as to cease from caring for separate souls. He hears the prayers of individuals (v. 35, end, O´), for the individual, as well as the nation, is under His eye. He is spoken of as raising up "the holy spirit" of a man (v. 45); as conferring the eldership, regarded as a divine institution (v. 50); as forbidding injustice (v. 53); as giving sentence to an angel to execute upon an individual (v. 55); as worthy to be praised for saving those who hope in Him (v. 61). A special Providence is recognised as watching over the destinies of separate souls; inspiring Daniel for a special effort; rescuing Susanna from a special danger. Heaven is regarded as the seat of the Divine Judge, towards which the innocent Susanna turned her eyes (v. 35), but from which the guilty Elders averted theirs (v. 9).

In v. 5 God is termed ὁ δεσπότης (*cf.* St. Luke ii. 29, Acts iv. 24); in vv. 24, 44, κύριος in vv. 55, 59 (Θ) θεός, for which O´ has κύριος, a word which it seems to prefer, as in i. 17, ii. 45, ix. 18. The fear of the Lord is evidently approved (v. 2), and instruction in the Law of Moses regarded as proper (v. 3), which is also referred to in vv. 33 and 62 (Θ only), and in act in v. 34. It would appear likely too that II. Sam. xxiv. 14 is quoted in v. 22 (Θ), Susanna in her strait borrowing the exclamation of David in his, and the words of both may well be contrasted with the idea of Hos. iv. 16b. Adultery is condemned as "sin before the Lord" (v. 23).

An angel is spoken of in vv. 44, 45 (O´ only) as giving a spirit of understanding to Daniel. The former verse might be taken to mean that he was visible.[48] He enabled Daniel to clear Susanna from her false accusation. An angel is also named in v. 55, in both versions, as likely to execute God's vengeance on the lying Elders. He is also mentioned in v. 62 of O´ as bringing a judgment of fire. This frequent mention of angels is quite in keeping with the canonical Daniel and other late books. And as E. Bunsen remarks, "the apocryphal doctrine about angels and evil spirits is sanctioned by the recorded doctrine of Christ" (*Hidden Wisd. of Christ*, 1865, I. 186). But it is singular that what has generally been considered the later recension should have less of it in this case than the earlier.

[48] καὶ ἰδοῦ ἄγγελος.

The description (v. 9) of the workings of conscience, while overt sin was under consideration, but before it was actually committed, shews a deep knowledge of the human heart, such as is found in the biblical writers. A process the reverse of 'turning unto God,' 'having the eyes unto Him' (II. Chron. xx. 12, Ps. xxv. 14), is very accurately depicted, as the dwelling upon some attractive lust is allowed to engage the mind. A better way of narrating such a matter it would be hard to devise.

Hippolytus, in his *Comm. on Dan.*, treats the whole story as having an allegoric meaning. Joacim represents Christ, Susanna the Christian Church; the bath represents Holy Baptism; and the two Elders the Jews and Gentiles persecuting the faithful (*D.C.B.* art. *Hippolytus*, p. 104a. For Christian sarcophagi with like symbolism, *see* 'Art'). M. de Castillo (Madrid, 1658) reflects in symbolism the increments of a later age when he sees in Susanna a type of the Virgin Mary—"Maria Virgo in illa figurata."

There does not appear to be anything 'Messianic' in this writing, unless Daniel himself be regarded as a type of Christ, executing just judgment, separating the righteous publicly from the wicked. There is also Origen's statement bearing upon this matter (*ad Afric.*, see *Speaker's Comm.* 327b), as to the prospect of becoming Messiah's mother, which the Elders held out to Susanna. St. Jerome, at the end of his *Commentary on Jeremiah*, has a slightly different version of their outrageous pretences.

Standing on surer ground than such speculations the theology of the piece itself is sound and proper.

CHRONOLOGY.

The period in which this trial befel Susanna is plainly that of the Babylonian Captivity, after the Jews were well settled in their conqueror's land, but not very long after.

The time covered by the narrative itself is obviously a very short one, probably only a few days at the outside.

If the suggestion in Julius Africanus' letter to Origen is correct, Joacim, Susanna's husband, was none other than Jehoiachin, the captive king of Judah. But Africanus is not by any means confident of this; nor does Hippolytus so identify them,[49] but contents himself with commenting on the statement of the text (v. 4) that Joacim was a very rich man. Nor is there anything in the Greek of either version to indicate his royalty, though the assertion that "he was more honourable than all others" fits in well with the notion. But if the story was coëval in its first form with the events narrated in it, the fact might be taken as universally known; or it might be thought politic to suppress it, as likely to be unpalatable to the reigning Babylonian monarch, in the written record. Thus it is possible to answer to a great extent Bissell's objection on v. 7, "that there seems to be no good reason why it should not have been definitely stated."

[49] In Hastings' *D.B.* art. *Jehoiachin*, it is stated that he does; but Hippolytus' *Comm.* in Migne, *Patr. gr.* x. 689, does not shew this. It is apparently based on a quotation from Hippolytus by Georgius Syncellus, given among the critical notes of Bonwetsch's ed. of *Hipp.* p. 10 (Lips. 1897).

His name is given as Ἰωακείμ both here, in II. Kings xxiv. 8, 12, and in I. Esd. i. 43, exactly the same as that of his father and predecessor Jehoiakim in I. Esd. i. 37 (39). Elsewhere the name is transliterated Ἰεχονίας and Ἰωαχίμ (Bar. i. 3, Jer. xxii. 24, *var. lect.*, II. Chron. xxxvi. 8, 9). In Judith iv. 6, xx. 8 we have Ἰωακείμ without variation, as the name of the high priest.

If this identification be correct the date must be subsequent to 597 B.C., the year of Jehoiachin's captivity; and probably not long after, since Daniel, who was taken to Babylon in or soon after the third year of Jehoiakim's reign in 603-4,[50] is represented as being still παιδάριον νεώτερον in v. 45. This phrase is somewhat tautologically rendered by A.V. as a 'young youth,' an instance which might be cited in support of the view that the English of the apocryphal was less excellent than that of the canonical books[51]; but, strange to say, the awkward expression is continued in R.V.

[50] But see G. Jahn, *in loc.*, and art. *Jehoiakim* in Hastings' *D.B.* as to making the date in Dan. i. 1 a little later.

[51] Scrivener, *Introd. to A.V.* § vii., and Sayce, *Tobit*, 1903, p. xvi.

Without necessarily implying it, v. 2 might easily be taken to convey the impression that Jehoiachin married in Babylon. Thus Hippolytus asserts, Ἰωακεὶμ πάροικος γενόμενος ἐν Βαβυλῶνι λαμβάνει τὴν Σωσάνναν εἰς γυναῖκα (Migne, *Patr. gr.* X. 689). And, on 'the same year' of v. 5, Reuss gives the interrogative note, "Im Jahre der Verheiratung des Joakim?"

If Susanna's husband really be Jehoiachin, he is the Jechonias who finds a place in the genealogy of Christ, St. Matt. i. 11, 12, Jehoiakim (Eliakim) being omitted. Bugati (*Dan.* p. 166) argues that Joakim is not Jehoiachin because of the name: "quo circa erroris arguendus est Jacobus Edessenus, sive auctor scholii ad calcem historiae Susannas adjecti in codice Parisiensi, qui Joacem virum Susannæ eum Joachin rege confundat." Bugati was probably unaware of the above-mentioned variations in the spelling of the name, which neutralize the force of his argument.

Two other doubtful indications of time are given by Hippolytus, viz. that Chelchias was Jeremiah's brother, making Susanna therefore his niece (Westcott's art. *Chelcias*, Smith's *D.B.*), and that 'a fit time' in v. 15 intimated the Feast of the Passover. Unsupported tradition and conjecture look like the grounds of these two indications respectively. Bardenhewer (*op. cit.* p. 75) not unreasonably deems that Hippolytus is thinking of Christian Baptism in connection with Easter, and so throws back the idea into the 'bath' and 'the fit time' of the Passover.

The Harklensian Syriac (W₂, Walton's second Syriac[52]) asserts both in vv. 1 and 45 that Daniel was twelve years old at the date of the story; also that Susanna was a widow after a married life of a few days only (v. 5), a statement to which neither Greek version lends any countenance. In fact, v. 63 (Θ) supposes Joakim to be alive at the end of the tale. Now we know from II. Kings xxv. 27 and Jer. xxviii. (xxxv.) 1-4 that Jehoiachin lived some years at least after his deportation. These Syriac insertions therefore as to Daniel's age and Susanna's widowhood are hardly compatible with one another on the supposition that she was the wife of Jehoiachin, king of Judah.

[52] *Speaker's Comm.*, end of *Introd. to Sus.*

It has been pointed out in the *Speaker's Commentary*, xlvib, that the insertion of 'twelve years old' into the text of the Syriac of Susanna may be due to "Christian re-handling," as also the extension of the final verse about Daniel's fame, "and he increased in favour with the family of Susanna," etc., so as to produce a correspondence with St. Luke ii. 42, 52. This is a possible theory, but one lacking, so far, the support of evidence. The condemnation of Susanna "at the ninth hour" (v. 41) might likewise be attributed to the same

Christian influence. This was no doubt operative here, as it was with Hippolytus.

In this connection it is worthy of note that in the longer recension of the "Ignatian" *Epist. ad Magnes.*, § III., Daniel is spoken of as δωδεκαετής when he γέγονε κάτοχος τῷ θείῳ πνεύματι, a phrase evidently reminiscent of the history of Susanna. Bishop Lightfoot notes on this: "His age is not given in the narrative, and it is difficult to see whence it could have been derived." He dates the longer Ignatian epistles in the second half of the 4th century (I. 246), while Thomas of Harkel lived in the 6th and 7th centres. But, though so much later, this Syriac translation may perhaps afford some clue to the ultimate discovery of Ignatius', or rather his expander's, source of information. The words παιδάριον νεώτερον do not of course necessarily imply such extreme youth as twelve years; nor are we in any way tied to the accuracy of this or other Harklensian variations.

Though this Addition therefore has its chronological difficulties, they need not be regarded as absolutely insurmountable.

CANONICITY.

Before the correspondence of Origen with Julius Africanus, whose letter is "a model of sober criticism" (Swete, *Patristic Study*, p. 56)—a correspondence renewed between Eusebius of Cæsarea and Porphyry[53], and between Rufinus and Jerome, with less sobriety—we have no record of the point having been mooted. For, as Bissell writes (p. 448), "We have no evidence that these pieces were not regarded as fully on a level with the remainder of the book." Africanus heard Origen use Susanna in controversy with one Bassus, and subsequently wrote to remonstrate, he himself being resident in Palestine. Some of his objections in this famous letter have considerable force, while others are very weak (*D.C.B.* I. p. 54b).

[53] *See* Jerome's *Pref. to Daniel*, end.

Origen deems Susanna part of the genuine Daniel, cut out by the Jews, as he suggests in his *Epistle* to Africanus. Bishop Gray (*O.T.* p. 612) describes this Epistle as 'suspected'; but it appears now to be generally accepted. Origen thinks that the motive of Susanna's exclusion was its relation of particulars discreditable to the Jewish nation. But the Bishop truly says, "there is no foundation for this improbable fancy." It is, however, maintained by Philippe in Vigouroux' *Dict.* (*cf.* 'Title and Position,' p. 109).

Origen also asserts the canonicity of Susanna in *Hom. in Levit.* § 1 (middle): "Sed tempus est nos adversus improbos presbyteros uti sanctæ Susannæ vocibus, quas illi quidem repudiantes, historiam Susannæ de catalogo divinorum voluminum desecrarunt. Nos autem et suscipimus, et opportune contra ipsos proferimus, dicentes 'Angustiæ mihi undique,'" etc. (v. 22).

Again, Origen refers to the matter in his *In Matthæum Commentariorum Series*. He quotes Daniel's words in v. 55, "angelus Domini habens gladium scindet te medium," and also "ausi sumus uti in hoc loco, Dan. exemplo, non ignorantes quoniam in Hebræo positum non est, sed quoniam in ecclesiis tenetur. Alterius autem temporis est requirere de huiusmodi" (Migne, *Patr. gr.* XIII. 1696). Delitzsch (*op. cit.* p. 103) says, on second thoughts, that he "adductum esse, ut ipsos libros apocryphos ab Origine pro γνησίοις et divinis habitos esse censeam."

About the same time, or probably a little earlier, St. Hippolytus (†230) gives a similar reason for the extrusion of this episode. He notes on v. 8, ταῦτα μὲν οὖν οἱ τῶν Ἰουδαίων ἄρχοντες βούλονται νῦν περικόπτειν τῆς βίβλου, φάσκοντες μὴ γενέσθαι ταῦτα ἐν Βαβυλῶνι· αἰσχυνόμενοι τὸ ὑπὸ τῶν πρεσβυτέρων κατ᾽ ἐκεῖνον τὸν καιρὸν γεγενημένον. On which Bardenhewer (*op. cit.* p. 76) remarks, "Susanna soll also früher auch in dem jüdischen Kanon gestanden haben und erst später (unliebsamen Vorwürfen gegenüber) aus demselben entfernt worden sein."

A. Scholz, however, who treats the book allegorically as a 'vision,' attributes early opinions adverse to its canonicity to the "Missverstehen der Erzählung und die unlösbaren Schwierigkeiten, die dieselbe bei der historischen Auffassung macht" (p. 139). The 'vision' theory, however, is a difficult one to maintain, serviceable though it may be in evading historic difficulties.

Lists of books of the canon do not help us much, as it is often uncertain whether 'Daniel' covers the Additions or not. We may safely conclude, however, that it does in Origen's own list, as preserved for us by Eusebius (*H.E.* VI. 25).

In the pseudo-Athanasius' *Synopsis sacr. script.* § 74, Susanna is named, after the books he deems canonical, as ἐκτὸς δὲ τούτων, along with four books of Maccabees and the Psalms of Solomon. In this case we might conclude that Δανιήλ does not cover Susanna; but in the beginning of the *Synopsis of Daniel* (§ 41) the story is mentioned as part of that book, and Bel and the Dragon, at the end, in the same way. This author's view, then, for and against the canonicity looks somewhat undecided. So in Cyril of Jerusalem's list in *Catech.* IV. § 35, 'Daniel' pretty certainly includes Susanna and probably the other two Additions, because in *Cat.* XVI. § 31, "de Spiritu sancto," he quotes Susanna 45 in company with Dan. iv. 6 as if on an equal footing.

It is quoted as Scripture before Origen's time by Irenæus IV. xxxv. 2, xli. 1; Tert. *de Cor. IV.*; Clem. Alex. *Proph. Ecl.* 1. Methodius, Bishop of Tyre, introduces Susanna into his Virgins' Songs as an example of brave sanctity, calling upon Christ[54] (see exact words under'Early Christian Literature,' p. 166).

[54] Warren, *Ante-Nicene Liturgy*, 1897, p. 188.

In the *Apost. Const.* II. 49, 'concerning accusers and witnesses,' this trial is instanced ὡς τοὺς δύο πρεσβυτέρους κατὰ Σωσάννης ἐν Βαβυλῶνι, and again in cap. 51 (Mansi, *Concil.* Florence, 1759, I. 352, 353).

Though Jerome (*Pref. to Dan.*) calls this and the other Additions 'fabulæ' (twice), it is pointed out by Peronne in his note to Corn. à Lap. on Dan. xiii. 1 (Paris, 1874) that Jerome uses the same word of the story of Samson (no ref. given), which he certainly regarded as canonical. He claims therefore that here it has "verum et nativum sensum vocis fabulæ, quæ quidem significat 'historiam, sermonem.'" But even if any disparaging sense could be eliminated from this particular word, Jerome's opinion is otherwise expressed.

The only possible reference to Susanna observable, I think, in the N.T. is in Matt, xxvii. 24, unless the name of Susanna in St. Luke viii. 3 be taken from our heroine's. It is of course emblematic of lily-like purity, and therefore very suitable for a woman. The story, with some omissions, forms the Epistle for Saturday after the third Sunday in Lent in the Sarum and Roman Missals.

Luther says that this and Bel are "beautiful and spiritual compositions, just as Judith and Tobias " (Bleek, *O.T.*, Venables' transl., 1869, II. 339).

In the Greek Church the Synods of Constantinople and Jerusalem in 1672 expressly decided, in opposition to Cyril Lucar and the Calvinists, that Susanna and Bel (with some other apocryphal books) were genuine elements of Divine Scripture, and denounced Cyril Lucar's conduct in styling them Apocrypha as ignorance or wickedness (Bleek, II. 343; Loisy, *O.T.* p. 243). The present Eastern Church reckons them, with the Song of the Three, canonical, as Bishop Nectarius expressly states (*Greek Manuals of Church Doctrine*, publ. by Eng. Ch. Assoc., Lond., 1901, p. 19). Also Bar-Hebræus (†1286), the Monophysite, comments on these fragments as if Holy Scripture (Loisy, p. 245). We see then that the testimonies to canonicity are of considerable strength, more so than is perhaps generally realised, even though the arguments to the contrary may be still stronger. The statement of Fritzsche (*Libri apocryphi*, 1871, p. xiii) is moderate and reasonable, fitting in well as it does with the views of our own Church, "Liber Danielis canonicus iam eo ipso tempore, quo primum in linguam græcam transferebatur, additamentis græcis auctus est, quorum tria maiora fere inde a seeulo quarto in eccl. christiana vulgo a viris doctis apocrypha iudicata sunt."

EARLY CHRISTIAN LITERATURE AND ART.

LITERATURE.

NEW TESTAMENT. In St. Matt. xxvii. 24 Pilate possibly adopts Daniel's words in v. 46, or at least accidentally falls in with them. In Heb. xi. 23 and Sus. 7 (O´) there is a strong similarity in the use of the word ἀστεῖος, as well as in Exod. ii. 2.

"Among names taken from the O.T., that of Susanna is not uncommon" (*D.C.A.* art. *Names*, 1374a). Not improbably therefore Susanna, in St. Luke viii. 3, may have been named after the Susanna of this history, as already mentioned under 'Canonicity,' p. 161. St. Susanna of the Roman Calendar, who is dated *circ.* 293, is most likely an example of this. She is not given an article in *D.C.B.*, but there is a short notice of her in *D.C.A.*, as commemorated in various Martyrologies on August 11th.

IRENÆUS (†200). In *Adv. Hær.*III. xlii. 1 there is an apparent reference to v. 55; in IV, xxxv. 2 to v. 42; and in IV. xli. 1, 'de presbyteris injustis,' vv. 20, 26 are quoted as "a Daniele propheta voces" in reproof of Christian presbyters. It is probable, too, that "Deum qui absconsa manifestat" (IV. xxxi. 2) may be a reminiscence of the phrase ὁ τῶν κρυπτῶν γνώστης in v. 42; and still more probably perhaps "qui est absconsorum cognitor" in IV. xxxv. 2 has its origin in this same verse.

CLEMENT or ALEXANDRIA (†220). In *Strom.* IV. (Heinsius' ed., Paris, 1629, p. 522) he speaks of Susanna and Miriam together, as if their biblical positions were on a par. In Hort and Mayor's edit. (1902) of *Strom.* VII. the words πρὸ τῆς γενέσεως in § 37 are referred to Susanna 43 (Θ); but it is hardly safe to assume that we have here more than an accidental approximation of wording.

HIPPOLYTUS (†230) distinctly recognizes Susanna at the end of his *Preface to Daniel*, as well as in his *Commentary* itself. This last, Bardenhewer (Freiburg im Breisgau, 1877, p. 69) deems, on account of its homiletic phrases, to be "Bruchstücke einer Homilie" (*cf.* art. *Hippolytus*, *D.C.B.* iii. 102a).

APOSTOLIC CONSTITUTIONS (third century?). Susanna's trial is instanced in II. 49, "Concerning accusers and witnesses" (*see* quotation under 'Canonicity,' p. 161), and again in cap. 51.

TERTULLIAN (†240). In *de Corona militis*, 4, after instancing Rebecca, he goes on to say of Susanna: "si et Susanna in iudicio revelata argumentum velandi præstat, possum dicere: et his velamen arbitrii fuit," etc. Also *de Pudic.* 17, etc.

ORIGEN (†254) frequently refers to Susanna in his commentaries, many references to which are collected by Schürer, *H.J.P.*, II. III. 186. In the middle of § 1 of his *Hom.* I. *in Levitic.* he quotes Susanna's words in v. 22 as if appropriate to the mouth of the book itself, surrounded, by those who doubted its canonicity (words quoted under 'Canonicity,' p. 158). In Eusebius' Præp. Ev. VI. 11, Origen is given as quoting v. 42 as a proof of God's foreknowledge, ἀπὸ τῶν γραφῶν τοῦτο παραστῆσαι. In his *Commentary* on St. John (bk. XX. § 5) he quotes v. 56 with ὡς ὁ Δανιὴλ φησι.

CYPRIAN (†258), in *Ep.* XLIII. 4, illustrates his remarks by a reference to "Susannam pudicam."

Bleek (*O.T.* II. 316) says that Bel and the Dragon and Susanna were used by both Irenæus and Cyprian in a similar way to the Scriptures of the Hebrew canon.

METHODIUS (†330), in his "Song of the Virgins" (II. 2). Ἄνωθεν, παρθένοι βοῆς, includes Judith and Susanna:

ὁρῶντες εἶδος εὐπρεπὲς, ὑφ᾽ ἧς
δύο κριταὶ Σουσάννας ἐμμανεῖς,
ἔρωτι λέξαν, Ὦ γύναι, κ.τ.λ.

(Migne, Patr. gr. XVIII. 212).

HILARY OF POITIERS (†367), *de Trin.* IV. 8 (Migne, *Patr. lat.* 10, 101), quotes Susanna 42, "Sicut beata Sus. dicit, Deus æternus absconditorum cognitor, sciens omnia," etc.

ATHANASIUS (†373) also, in his *Disc, against Arians*, I. 13, quotes this popular verse (42) as "in Daniel." In the *Life of Anthony*, § 43, he refers to Susanna, as well as in the 'doubtful' *Synopsis S.S.*

EPHREM SYRUS (†378) refers both in his *Ep. ad Johann. monachum*, and in his 15th *Parænesis*, to the blessed Susanna.

GRATIAN (†383) notes on Can. XI. of Neocæsarea (315 A.D.) in *Decreta* I. 78, c. iv., "Daniel, we read, received the spirit of prophecy before he had arrived even at youth." The Canon itself, as given by Hefele, makes no mention of Daniel.

CYRIL OF JERUSALEM (†386) refers (*Catech.* I. 31) to Daniel's inspiration to rescue Susanna, and quotes v. 45 with γέγραπται γάρ.

GREGORY OF NYSSA (†396) quotes, in his *Hexaëmeron* (Migne, *Patr. gr.* XLIV. p. 71) and in his *Making of Man*, v. 42, twice as a prophetic writing (XXIX. 1).

AMBROSE (†397) has, Sermons XLIX. and L., "de accusato Domino apud Pilatum et de Susanna," in which he draws a parallel between them, as to silence under false charges, at considerable length (Basel, ed. 1527, III. 549).

SULPICIUS SEVERUS (†400?), in his *Hist. Sacr.* lib. II. § 1, gives an outline of the story of Susanna, after the events of Dan. i. and before those of chap, ii., evidently regarding it as historical.

CHRYSOSTOM (†407) has a sermon "de Susanna," in which he compares her to the "garden enclosed" of Solomon's Song iv. 12 (quoted in Arnald's *Commentary*).

JEROME (†420), in his *de Nominibus Hebraicis*, includes, under the Book of Daniel, Susanna and Joacim without any distinction from the names in the rest of the book (ed. Vallarsi, vol. III.).

AUGUSTINE (†430) draws, in *de Civ. Dei*, I. 19, a parallel between Susanna and Lucretia, greatly to the advantage of the former. Arnald, on v. 23, gives some extracts from this.

CYRIL OF ALEXANDRIA (†444) quotes v. 56 at least twice, viz. on Hos. xii. 8 and on Zeph. i. 11. In the latter case he speaks of it as παρὰ γε τοῖς ἱεροῖς γράμμασιν, giving it thus explicitly a high position.

THEODORET (†457) quotes in Letter CX., Susanna 22; but in his comment on Daniel, Susanna is not contained.

MAMERTUS CLAUDIANUS (†474). The following occurs in a hymn attributed to this writer, "*In Jacobum magistrum equitum*," but which Migne says is 'dubiæ auctoritatis': "Sic tibi det vires sancta Susanna suas."

NICEPHORUS OF CONSTANTINOPLE (†828) classes Susanna among his "antilegomena." As he makes no separate mention in his lists of the Song, or of Bel and the Dragon, he presumably reckons them under 'Daniel'[55] (Migne, *Patr. gr.* c. 1056). At the end of pseudo-Athanasius' *Synopsis S.S.* comes a list of κανονιζόμενα, so similar to Nicephorus' list in order and contents as to suggest that they had some close connection; and it is possible that this appendage may be of even later date than the Synopsis itself, which may be attributed to the 6th century (Loisy, *A.T.*, p. 147).

[55] But Δανιὴλ ψευδεπίγραφα may refer to them.

The above are specimens of the numerous references made to Susanna by early Christian writers, both Greek and Latin, who evidently found in her a favourite instance to adduce in support of their teaching. Nor ought we, in such a matter, to treat lightly the tenor of Christian antiquity so remarkably manifested.

ART.

From early times scenes from Susanna were often chosen for artistic treatment. In "a list of the symbols most frequently represented in painting or sculpture by the Church of the first seven centuries" Susanna is included (*D.C.A.* art. *Symbolism*).

Frescoes of Susanna and the Elders occur, though not with great frequency, in the Catacombs (*D.C.A.* I. art. *Fresco*, 700a). W. Lowrie, in his *Christian Art* (N.Y. and Lond. 1901, p. 210), mentions a second-century fresco of Susanna and the Elders judged by Daniel, in the cemetery of Callistus; also he says, "in the Capella græca in St. Priscilla the story is depicted with unusual dramatic interest in several scenes." Three old Italian sarcophagi have bas-reliefs of Susanna and the Elders as emblematic of the Church enduring persecution; others are known in southern Gaul (*D.C.A.* art. *Church, Symbols of*). A woodcut is given in this article of a sheep (ewe?) between two wild beasts (wolves?), 'Susanna' and 'Senioris' being written over them respectively, the artist evidently fearing that the symbolism might otherwise not be perceived.

Scenes from the history of Susanna carved on sarcophagi are more frequent in France than in Italy. It has been thought that the two Elders may be taken to represent the two older forms of religion, the Pagan and the Jewish (*D.C.A., O.T. in Art*, II. 1459b). In the same Dict. (*Sculpture*, II. 1867a) it is noted that the cycle of subjects has a remarkable correspondence with those named in the Roman Breviary "Ordo commendationis animæ," where "Libera, Dom. animam servi tui sicut liberasti Sus. de falso crimine," is one of the petitions.

It is fair to presume that Delitzsch refers to some of the above when he writes, "Susannæ historia in sarcophagis veterum Christianorum cum sacris historiis insculpta conspicitur" (*op. cit.* 26).

In the Brit. Mus., 2nd North Gallery, Room V., there is a glass fragment of the 4th century, found at Cologne, representing (probably) Susanna amongst other subjects. She also appears on a carved ivory reliquary of Brescia, which is most likely not later in date than 800 (*D.C.A.* art. *Reliquary*, II. 1780b).

In the Byzantine Guide to Painting (Ἑρμηνεία τῆς ζωγραφικῆς), given in Didron's *Christian Iconography* (Bohn's ed., Lond. 1886, I. 45*n*, II. 284), 'Daniel defends Susanna' is put immediately after the scene in Dan. i. 15, and before the other scenes given out of Daniel (*cf.* 'Position,' p. 109). Didron's MS. of this work is probably of the 15th century, though the monks of Athos, whence it appears to have come, regarded it as some five centuries older.

There is a window of stained glass, said to be *cinque-cento*, in the westernmost bay of the south aisle of St. James' Church, Bury St. Edmunds, of which the three lower lights represent the trial of Susanna. In the centre Susanna's bath takes the form of a deep font, in which she is standing. The Elders are clothed in purple.[56]

[56] There is a very quaint note in Gwillim's *Heraldry* (1611, p. 109) as to a mulberry figured on a shield, "This fruit hath a purple blushing colour, in the one resembling the judges' attire who attempted Susanna, in the other that hue of their face which should have been in them, if they had been so gracious to blush at their fault," etc.

In Sumner's *Antiquities of Canterbury*, 1703, the second figure in the third window of the cathedral is described as "Daniel in medio seniorum," and this inscription is given:

"Mirantur pueri seniores voce doceri
Sic responsa dei sensum stupent Pharasæi."

(Reprinted in *Ancient Glass Painting*, by an Amateur, Oxf. 1848, p. 355.)

In the scheme of stained glass for Truro cathedral there are several apocryphal subjects, including a window in the south-east transept having "Susanna and the Mother of the Seven Martyrs" for its subjects (Donaldson, *Bishopric of Truro*, 1902, App. V.).

A carved chimney-piece exists in Chillingham Castle, Northumberland, representing Susanna and the Elders (Murray, *Handbook to Northumberland*, 1873, p. 326).

This scene has been a wonderfully popular one with painters. Altdorfer, Carracci, Correggio, A. Coypel, van Dyck, Guercino, Rembrandt, Rubens, Santerre, Tintoretto, Valentin, and P. Veronese may be named amongst those who have treated it. A picture entitled 'Susanna' was exhibited in the Royal Academy, London, in 1886, by Fred. Goodall, R.A.

Thus we see that the many picturesque incidents in this Addition have not been overlooked by Christian artists in search of subjects for the brush or the chisel. Of these three supplementary sections of Daniel the History of Susanna has, in this respect, been found much the most suggestive; probably as the one which is thought to contain the highest passion and feeling.

"EXAMPLE OF LIFE AND INSTRUCTION OF MANNERS."

In the character of *Susanna* we see unconquerable *Purity* in thought and deed; prayerful *Trust* in God under a false and cruel accusation,[57] and, in the face of death, securing deliverance from an unexpected quarter (*cf.* v. 60 with II. Cor. i. 10). With v. 55 Hippolytus compares Tob. iii. 2 (Vulgate). The parallels drawn by St. Chrysostom and St. Augustine will be found under 'Early Christian Literature,' p. 167. Susanna's trouble may be taken as a conspicuous illustration of Ps. xxxiv. 19.

·[57] There are similar instances in chaps. iii. and vi. of the canonical·
Daniel. See also the *Notes on Scripture, in loco, of* Bishop Wilson, of Sodor
and Man, who tells what comfort he derived from hearing Susanna read
in the daily service when himself falsely accused.

Susanna was conscientious as well as pure; would not lie, being tenderly
nurtured morally as well as physically.[58] She had the virtue of bodily
cleanliness as well as social purity, and affords an early instance of the use of
the prepared bath.

·[58] Thackeray's mention of Susanna in *Tht Newcomes*, chap, lvi., seems·
pointless, though that in chap. xix. is suitable enough. Steele has an absurd
reference in the *Spectator*, No. 14, to the "opera of Susanna, or Innocence
Betrayed, which will be exhibited next week, with a pair of new Elders."·

It is noticeable, too, that no unfavourable traits develop themselves on the
re-establishment of her happiness and the condemnation of her slanderers;
there is no excessive reaction to unbecoming laxity, no ἄσχημον πρᾶγμα.

In the character of the *Elders* we see judicial position and feigned piety used
as a cloak for lust and slander; great hardness of heart in condemning Susanna
to death, with the full knowledge that she was innocent; unblushing
effrontery (v. 50); sins of the tongue in 'lying and slandering.'

Hooker (*Ecc. Pol.* V. 2) refers, according to the marginal note (though they
are not named in the text), to these Elders as examples of "affected atheism,"
"where the windows of the soul are of very set purpose closed"; "they turned
away their mind and cast down their eyes, that they might not see heaven nor
remember just judgments." St. Hippolytus on v. 61 quotes Prov. xxvi. 27 very
appositely. The fall of the Elders shews the need for our Lord's order in St.
Matt. v. 28, and the terrible results of acting otherwise.

The individual character of each Elder has a little light thrown upon it by the
form of condemnation framed by Daniel. That of the first is chiefly based on
his unjust judgment, that of the second on his lewd conduct, each judgment
being varied in this way according to the form of his previous iniquities. The
knowledge which Daniel possessed of these appropriately determined the
cast of his sentence. That he had some acquaintance with their former habits
is shewn by vv. 52, 53, 56.

The change to the plural in v. 57 is difficult to explain, and does not receive
attention at the hands of the commentators; in fact Ball applies this verse,
without mentioning the change of number, to the one Elder only. Although
these godless judges failed in accomplishing their purpose, they were not on
this account less scandalous betrayers of virtue.

In Susanna's *Servants* we see fidelity, sympathy, and no eagerness to believe an ill report. As regards Susanna, this fact speaks volumes for the excellence of her conduct.

In *Daniel* we see the courage and penetrating acumen which are so characteristic of his whole career, impressing all with whom he was brought into contact. He weighs a matter carefully before coming to a decision. By unmasking hypocrisy and securing justice he is delighted to set right a grievous wrong.[59] He appears as the best judge (*cf.* the estimation shewn of the justice of God by Azarias, Song of the Three, 4-8). Daniel further exhibits a decision and an absence of self-distrust, in undertaking tasks of great risk, quite in accordance with his character as portrayed in the canonical book, and in Bel and the Dragon. In each case he is alert, acute, and fearless; his conduct in different circumstances is quite in keeping with itself. Using his talents thoroughly, he makes "full proof of his ministry."

[59] St. Antony of Padua curiously gives vv.. 52, 56, as an example of the "Zeal of prelates" (*Moral Concordance*, Neale's edit., n.d., p. 105).

There is a strong resemblance in ideas, though not much in words, between Daniel's sentence in v. 55 and St. Matt. xxiv. 51. The judgment of Daniel in this case may be taken as a type of the Last Judgment, correcting the unjust judgments of this world.

A high value is set on Scripture, as v. 53 shews, where it is quoted as an authoritative rule of conduct; v. 5, too, if it is to be regarded as a reference to Jer. xxix. 23, points to a similar high esteem for it as the word of the Lord. Susanna herself in v. 22 evidently remembers David's words in II. Sam. xxiv. 14, when he too had to make his choice between falling into the hand of the Lord or the hand of man, thus shewing her ready knowledge of the O.T.

Much admirable moral teaching therefore may be drawn from the characters of this little work of world-wide interest, teaching which is needed in all nations and in all periods.

PART IV
THE HISTORY OF BEL AND THE DRAGON

תִּרְמֹס כְּפִיר וְתַגִּין
(תהל׳ צא׳ יג׳)

THE HISTORY OF BEL AND THE DRAGON.

ANALYSIS.

v.

1, 2. Introduces Cyrus and Daniel.

3. How Bel was worshipped by the Babylonians.

4-7. Discussion as to Bel's worship[60] between the King and Daniel.

8, 9. The King enquires of Bel's priests, and says that they or Daniel must die.

10-14. The test agreed upon to prove whether Bel partook of the offerings or no.

15-22. Decided in the negative by discovery of the Priests' trick, who are slain and their idol destroyed.

23. Introduces the other object of worship[60], the Dragon.

24-27. Conversation as to its divinity between the King and Daniel, who, with the former's permission, ingeniously slays it.

28, 29. Anger of the Babylonians with them both.

30-32. They cause Daniel to be cast into the lions' den.

33-40. He is miraculously saved by Habakkuk.

40, 42. The King acknowledges the Lord, sets Daniel free, and delivers his persecutors to the fate intended for the prophet.

> [60] In each case it is not clear from the text that the 'worship' consisted in anything else than supplying food.

[Endnote: N.B.—It is unaccountable why the 'heading' in A.V. *begins* with v. 19. *Cf.* Sus. for a similar peculiarity.]

TITLE AND POSITION.

TITLE.

Βὴλ καὶ Δράκων is the usual title of this booklet. It is obviously derived from the names of the two idols destroyed in the two portions of the story. But Cod. Chis. has the curious heading, Ἐκ προφητείας Ἀμβακοὺμ υἱοῦ Ἰησοῦ ἐκ τῆς φυλῆς Λευί (*cf.* v. 33). The Syriac also has the equivalent of this. In some

Syriac MSS. 'Dragon' is given as a separate title before v. 23; and Luther's version, at the same point, expands this into 'von Drachen zu Babel.'

In Codd. A, Q, the entire piece is headed ὅρασις ιβ΄, and is thus treated as an integral part of Daniel, finishing the book, the 12th chapter of which ends in Cod. A with ὅρασις ια΄.[61] In B it follows, if possible, still more closely, there being no intermediate heading[62], In Cod. A, at the end, there is τέλος Δαν. προφήτου, which, except in the case of Ruth, is not A's usual way of terminating works. The Arabic Version in Walton also superscribes it as a 'vision' (Scholz, p. 139).

[61] The title ὅρασις is also used in Q in some of Isaiah's visions, *e.g.* xvii. 1.

[62] *See* under Theodoret in 'Early Christian Literature,' and 'Chronology,' p. 224.

The title 'the book of the little Daniel' seems applied to Bel and the Dragon in a Nestorian list mentioned by Churton (p. 389), and seemingly in Ebed Jesu's list of Hippolytus' works (*D.C.B.* art. *Hippolytus*, III. p. 104a). This title, which usually belongs to Susanna, when applied to Bel and the Dragon, must refer, not to Daniel's age, but to the size of the book. Delitzsch (*op. cit.* 25n) mentions, without further description, one MS. from Mount Athos which entitles it περὶ τοῦ Ἀββακούμ.

The source of the marginal reading of A.V. "Bel's Dragon" (also given in the title to Susanna) does not appear to be identified.

POSITION.

As to the place of this piece in some of the Greek MSS. *see* above.

Professor A. Scholz (*Judith und Bel und der Drache*, Würzburg, 1896, p. 200) finds fault with Holmes and Parsons for having disturbed the position of this book without offering sufficient indication of having done so: "die Stücke willkürlich versetzt sind."

In the Vulgate it is reckoned as chap. xiv. of Daniel, coming after Susanna, which forms chap. xiii., as also in the Hexaplar Syriac. Caj. Bugati, in his edition of this text, regards its ascription to Habakkuk as a reason for its detached position at the end (*see* 'Authorship,' p. 186).

J. Fürst's idea (quoted by Bissell, p. 444), that the work was originally incorporated in chap. vi., seems far less likely than his conjecture with regard to the position of Susanna (*q.v.*). Indeed, except for a certain similarity in the lions' den miracle, it is not easy to see why it should be joined to any part of chap. vi. Nor do the similar points of the den incidents seem any real ground for making one story follow directly upon the other.

E. Philippe (Vigouroux *Dict.* II. 1266) attempts, rather feebly, to account for its omission from the Hebrew Bibles. He says, "elle parut à tort aux Juifs faire double emploi avec un récit pareil, VI." This seems to be a gratuitous supposition of no great probability.

As the story deals with the latter part of Daniel's life, its place at the conclusion of the book is very fitting. In Cod. A the subscription mentioned above, marking it as the "end of Daniel the prophet," distinctly attaches it to the Book of Daniel, and precludes further additions. On the whole, if its connection with the Book of Daniel is to be recognized, this position at the close may be regarded as the most suitable.

AUTHORSHIP.

In Θ, Bel and the Dragon is apparently assumed to be by the same writer as the rest of the Book of Daniel. So in *Breshith Rabbah*[63] on Gen. xxxvii. 24 we have nearly the words of v. 28 *sq.*, introduced by "This is as it is written in Daniel" (Ball, 344a). In Raymund Martini's *Pugio fidei* (Paris, 1651, p. 740) the Aramaic is given as בדניאל (*see* under 'Chronology,' p. 229).

[63] This has been attributed to Rabba bar Nachman of Pumbaditha, about A.D. 300, but is probably later. *See*, however, Etheridge, *Jerus. and Tiberias*, p. 143.

If, however, it be presumed that Daniel is not the author, we are left without any clue to the writer's name, except what is afforded us by the LXX title, which treats the piece as an extract from a prophecy of Habakkuk, son of Jesus. Most probably the minor prophet of that name is intended, though this has been doubted on chronological and on genealogical grounds; and the position of Bel and the Dragon in the MSS. lends no countenance to a connection with Habakkuk's prophecy. Rothstein nevertheless, in Kautzsch, *Apocr.* (p. 178), regards it as certain that the minor prophet is meant; and so likewise do Schürer and Driver in their articles in Hauck's *Encyclopædia* (I. 639), and in Hastings' *D.B.* respectively; and Keil, who is referred to below (p. 188).

Still, it is curious that a Levite of the name of Jesus, who had sons, is mentioned in I. Esd. v. 58, and elsewhere in the same book. Further evidence, however, which might connect him with the LXX title, is not forthcoming. But it is noticeable that in Hab. ii. 18 *sq.* idolatry, probably Chaldean, is scoffed at in a tone not dissimilar to that of this work.

Eusebius and Apollinarius, in controversy with Porphyry, accept this title as correct (Churton, 390b). So Bugati (Milan, 1788, p. 163) treats the authorship of Habakkuk as the reason of the detached position of the fragment at the end of the book. Hesychius of Jerusalem, quoted under 'Early Christian Literature,' declines to express an opinion as to the identity of Habakkuk. The *Synopsis sacr. Script.*—referred to by Ball (350b) and Bissell (447) as if a genuine work of Athanasius—perhaps affords ground for a third theory. For it makes mention (after N.T. books, § 75) of a certain pseudo-epigraphic writing of Ἀμβακούμ which might perhaps be the προφητεία named in the LXX title. All things considered, the theory that the well-known prophet Habakkuk was meant by LXX seems the most probable.

But if Bel and the Dragon be merely the crystallization of what is called a 'fluid myth,' or traditional floating story, its original authorship is not merely unknown, but is undiscoverable, and was probably a doubtful matter even to those who first rendered it into Greek. This view accounts too, as nothing else seems satisfactorily to do, for the many changes, insertions, and omissions in different versions. Such stories, at any rate in their earlier days, are subject to variation in many points as the result of oral repetition. Still, the 'fluidity' of this piece is by no means so great as that of Tobit, where the variations are on a much wider scale.

If the 'fluid myth' theory be accepted, the original becomes an anonymous story, built up on the renown of Daniel, a piece of Haggadah in fact, as some, not unreasonably, have ventured to think; such as J.W. Etheridge, who classes these pieces under that head, or, as he styles them, "histories coloured with fable" (*Jerusalem and Tiberias*, Lond. 1856, p. 109). Reuss regards it as still more imaginative, deeming all except the temple to be "reine Erfindung, und zwar eine ziemlich geistlose" (*O.T.* VII. 269). But Prof. Sayce thinks that "the author was better acquainted with Babylon and Babylonian history than the other apocryphal writers" (*Temple Bible*, 'Tobit,' etc., Lond. 1903, pp. xiv, 95).

Furthermore it must be remembered that even if Bel and the Dragon was added to Daniel as an appendix by a later hand, there may still be truth in the story; its erroneousness is not necessarily proved, nor is it needful to assume, as is sometimes done, that all its events are fictitious. This seems to be done by G.H. Curteis (S.P.C.K. *Comm.*, 'Introd. to Hab.'), who writes: "The absurd legends with which the Rabbis and the author of Bel and the Dragon amused themselves are not worthy of serious attention." And Keil also, in his *Commentary on the Minor Prophets*, while accepting the superscription of Cod. Chis. as supporting Habakkuk's Levitic origin, regards the rest of the legend as "quite worthless" (Clark's translation, pp. 49, 50). So, too, W.J. Deane (*Pulpit Bible*, 1898, 'Hab.' p. 111) says, "The whole account is plainly unhistorical, and its connection with the canonical writer cannot be maintained for a moment."

Supposing the story to be true, however, it may form an instance, both at its outset and its close, of what is recorded in Dan. vi. 28, of Daniel prospering in the reign of Cyrus the Persian. But, in the present state of our knowledge, speculations lead to no positive result, for the real author cannot be determined.

DATE AND PLACE OF WRITING.

DATE.

The idea, which may be a true one, that this is the latest of these three appendices, seems chiefly founded on its position at the end of Daniel, and on its subject-matter, which contains indications of belonging to the prophet's latter years. Having passed safely through many trials, he now boldly laughs at the idols of Babylon (vv. 7, 19). His contempt is unconcealed, and he again confidently risks his life for the true God. In v. 19 we also find him venturing to hold the king back—ἐκράτησεν τὸν βασιλέα (Θ). Long experience in surmounting great difficulties by divine help had strengthened his nerve and confirmed his faith.

Original. If the LXX be taken as a translation, the original is of course older than the Greek text, but not necessarily much older. If the statement at the head, however, be accepted as referring to Habakkuk the prophet, the original is of course thrown back to a much earlier date, say *circ.* 600 B.C., and Hebrew, not Aramaic, would be the language. But this theory will scarcely commend itself to many (*cf.* 'Chronology,' p. 223).

LXX. There seems no reason to doubt that Bel and the Dragon always formed a part of this Greek version of Daniel. Pusey (quoted in Churton, *Uncan. and Apocr. Script,* p. 389) speaks of it as 'contemporary with the LXX,' while Rothstein (Kautzsch, 178, 9) attributes it to the second century B.C., being probably of the same date as Susanna.

Theodotion. This version may reasonably be assigned to the second century A.D. But it has been pretty clearly shewn that Theodotion worked up some Greek version other than the LXX. Many of the quotations from Daniel in the N.T., and especially those in Revelation (specified in *D.C.B.* art. *Theodotion,* IV. 975b), shew that a version largely corresponding with his existed at the time when these quotations were made. The Book of Baruch also (same art. 976a) bears evidence of the employment of this Theodotionic ground-version, the origin of which is at present unknown. In this connection compare Prof. Swete's *Introd. to Greek O.T.* ed. 2, p. 48, and Schürer's pointed saying, quoted there in note (3), "Entweder Th. selbst ist älter als die Apostel, oder es hat einen 'Th.' vor Th. gegeben." There seems little reason to doubt that the unnamed previous version extended to this and the other Additions to Daniel.

PLACE.

Original (Semitic?). Babylonia, or possibly Palestine. " The writer," says Bissell on v. 2, "shews a familiar acquaintance with what was the probable state of things in Babylon when the event narrated is supposed to have occurred."

Of the things mentioned, clay is common in Babylonia, and brass or bronze was used as a material for images; and the lion was an inhabitant of the country.

There is no sign (in this piece) of Hellenic thought influencing Jewish belief, such as would have been likely to shew itself in a purely Alexandrian production. The strong hatred of idolatry is quite in accordance with a Babylonish origin; more so perhaps than with an Alexandrian. *Cf.* Jer. xliv. 8, which seems to shew that, at any rate in the early days of the dispersion in Egypt, the severance from idolatry was not so sharp as in Babylonia.

The mention of pitch (v. 27) as a readily obtainable commodity is inconclusive, as stated under the corresponding section of Part II. The possible confusion between זצפא (storm-wind) and זיפא (pitch), pointed out by Marshall in his article on Bel and the Dragon in Hastings' *Dict.*, does not look probable as occurring in a list of substances of this kind.

LXX. Alexandria may be pretty certainly named. What Bishop Westcott calls "an Alexandrine hand" (*D.B.* I. p. 448 ed. 1, 714 ed. 2) has been generally deemed apparent. So Bissell says: "The contents furnish tolerably safe evidence of its Egyptian origin." But this does not seem to agree very well with his note on v. 2, quoted at the beginning of this chapter.

It might have been thought that the weights and measures which enter into this story in v. 3 of both versions, and in v. 27 of LXX, would have afforded some valuable local indications. But unfortunately for this requirement, the weights and measures of the ancient world were so much assimilated as to yield, in the question before us, no certain clue. Alexandria too, being a great commercial centre, had become somewhat syncretistic. As P. Smith remarks, in his article *Mensura*, in *D. Gk. & Rom. A.* (1872, p. 754b), "The Roman system, which was probably derived from the Greek, agreed with the Babylonian both in weights and measures." It is stated, however, in Hastings' *D.B.* (IV. 911b, 913b) that ἀρτάβαι and μετρηταί were identified at Alexandria, in which case they may have been used here as rough equivalents for the translation of some Semitic words, such as חֹמֶר and סְאָה in Isai. v. 10 and I. Kings xviii. 32 respectively. The μνᾶ of v. 27 is also both Babylonian and Alexandrian (*see* Hastings' *D.B.* iv. 904a). The signs, from this source, of local origin must not therefore be pressed.

Theodotion. From what little we know of this translator's life, it is not improbable that he made his version at Ephesus.

The genitive form μαχαίρης in v. 26, thought to be Ionic, may lend a little support to this. *Cf.* Heb. xi. 34, Rev. xiii. 14, in A; B here failing; yet it is found in B, by the first corrector, in St. Luke xxi. 24. But *cf.* Swete's *Introd.* p. 304. On the other hand, the use of σώματα in v. 32 (Θ only) for 'slaves' is given by Deissmann (p. 160) as an example of Egyptian usage. It is found in Gen. xxxiv. 29, Tob. x. 10, and elsewhere. Its use by Polybius (mentioned without reference by Deissmann) does not give us much 'local' assistance, for his travels were so extensive that he may have picked it up in various places. But its occurrence in Rev. xviii. 13 may suggest that it was in use at Ephesus also. Deissmann (p. 117) also thinks ἐδαπανῶντο εἰς (v. 3) to be an Alexandrian idiom; but in the same verse we find the spelling ῥάκουτα, which is considered by Liddell and Scott to be an Ionic form. The indications therefore of this linguistic kind nearly counterbalance one another.

FOR WHOM AND WITH WHAT OBJECT WRITTEN.

This story was evidently composed for Jewish use, not improbably for Jews who had returned from the Captivity, as a popular memorial of Babylonish days. And perhaps the general tenor of the piece implies that it was written to serve, not so much to convert idolaters, as for the encouragement of those who were striving, or had striven, to maintain the faith among the heathen. Its tone and subject make its composition in the first instance for Babylonian Jews, or Palestinian Jews returned from captivity, more likely than for their Alexandrian brethren. To these latter, however, it soon found its way. But it is amongst Christian people that this narrative has had its longest and deepest influence. The more it was valued by Christians the less it seemed regarded by Jews. In this respect its fate was similar to that of the entire LXX.

A distinct moral purpose is not obscurely indicated by the trend of the whole story. It is not merely a record of two interesting episodes in the prophet's later days, but it also aims at a definite religious object. That object is to throw contempt on idolatry, whether directed to inanimate or animate things; to honour Daniel as vindicator of the true worship; and to shew that the adoration of heathen deities is lying and deceptive, and ought to be supplanted by that of the Lord.

It is evidently desired to put both idols and idolaters into ridiculous positions, not for mere amusement, but in order to destroy the confidence which was groundlessly placed in them. The weapons of sarcasm and contemptuous treatment are used with success, even as Elijah employed them on Baal and his worshippers at an earlier time (I. Kings xviii. 27). A desire to convert the heathen, by proving the absurdity of their idol-worship, may be inferred from the last clause of v. 27, compared with vv. 5, 25. As the history of Susanna deals with errors of Jewish practice, so does this writing with the errors of heathenism.

The providence of God in protecting those who suffer for His sake is clearly inculcated in the latter portion of the work. A sense of this would, with other results, give confidence in the fight against idolatry; the more needed because Bel was evidently a very popular deity with high and low, and difficult to dislodge. The frequent compounding of 'Bel' with proper names (Belshazzar and Belteshazzar)[64] shews the regard in which he was held. Compare the similar compounding of 'Jehovah' amongst the Jews. But, although Bel was deemed a beneficent deity, being, as Gesenius calls him (s.v. בֵּל sub בָּצַל), 'agathodemon, omnis felicitatis auctor,' Daniel does not spare him on that account. Thomas "Wintle[65] suggests that the image in chap. iii. "was Bel, or some of the Assyrian deities, as we may collect from iii. 14"; and Bar-Hebræus' notion that the gift of Bel to Daniel, in v. 22 of our story, was in order that he might be rewarded by the gold with which the image was plated, agrees well enough with iii. I (Berlin, 1888, p. 28).

[64] Schrader, *Cuneiform Inscriptions of O.T.*² II. 125, considers Bel not to enter explicitly into the second of these names, which he takes to mean 'may his life protect'; but even in this case the mention of a Deity is evidently understood. But *cf.* Dan. iv. 8. Gesenius and Longfield (*Chaldee Grammar*, 1859, p. 115) take the older view. *See* also Sayce's art. in Hastings' *D.B.* on *Merodach-Baladan*, where M. seems identified with Bel; also art. *Merodach*.

[65] *Daniel*, Oxf. 1792, p. 40.

The aim is to depict Daniel, distinguished for his wisdom and piety, as the successful, though sorely tried, opponent of heathenism, and as the representative of the Living God. His character to a great extent resembles that pourtrayed in the rest of the work bearing his name. It is shewn how he continued to face and to solve the difficult problems of court life in Babylon. And albeit he secured no small measure of fame, and perhaps of popularity, at the time, these earthly results, in their abiding form, it has lain with posterity to give him.

On the supposition that Alexandria was the birthplace of the piece, it has been suggested that the aim of the writer was "to warn against the sin of idolatry some of his brethren who had embraced Egyptian superstition."[66] But no special reference to Egyptian forms of idolatry is apparent in support of this view, which seems based on little more than a wish to fit in the idolatry with the theory of the story having an Alexandrian origin.

[66] *Chambers's Encyclop.*, 1888, art. *Bel.*

A. Scholz's notion that the whole piece is a 'vision' with allegoric or apocalyptic meanings only, and never intended to be taken as history, looks like a wonderfully forced hypothesis, laying a great strain on the imaginations both of the writer and the reader. The book having been received as canonical in the Roman communion, its contents must at all hazards be reconciled with the maintenance of that position. Yet it is fair to note that Luther, on other grounds, regarded Susanna and Bel and the Dragon as pretty spiritual fictions, in which history must take its chance (Zöckler, p. 216).

INTEGRITY AND STATE OF THE TEXT.

This double story seems to have been treated as one in the Greek. In the Syriac and Arabic versions the Dragon has a separate title (noticed in A.V. margin, "Some add this title *of the Dragon*'). The former, strangely enough, has 'end of Daniel' before this title. And in the Syro-Chaldee version, given in Midrash *Rabbah de Rabbah*, Bel has a subscription, and the Dragon a fresh title (*see* Ball, 345a).

In v. 23 ἐν τῷ αὐτῷ τόπῳ (O´) are wanting as connecting words in B, but the reference to Bel in v. 28 serves to consolidate the two portions of the story. A and Q also, as well as correctors of B, have an additional clause in v. 24, which pre-supposes the former portion of the piece, a clause given in A.V. and R.V. The καὶ of μὴ καὶ τοῦτον in O´ answers the same purpose. Daniel's mocking tone at the end of v. 27 agrees well with his sense of humour in v. 7. Cyrus' ready compliance, too, in v. 26 is only accounted for fully by the shock given to his idolatrous beliefs in the Bel part of the story. And so far the internal evidence argues for the unity of the piece. But it is noticeable that the Epistle for Tuesday after the Fifth Sunday in Lent in the Sarum and Roman Missals consists of the Dragon story only, beginning at v. 29, with some slight introductory changes.

And Gaster's recovered Aramaic text (which he believes to have been the basis of Theodotion's Greek) consists of the Dragon story only. The notion that it had a separate currency is therefore, to a certain extent, supported; and this would still be the case, even if Gaster's text is not an original, but a translation.

If Gaster's Aramaic were really the basis of Θ's version, it would follow that he did not confine himself to making a mere recension of the O´ text, though he evidently availed himself of it as far as he thought proper. It is highly probable that this would apply to the Bel as well as to the Dragon story, although the corresponding Aramaic of the former is not at present forthcoming.

Neither the Ο΄ nor Θ's original text seem to have been materially tampered with, either in the way of addition or omission. Each has some clauses not contained in the other: Ο΄ in vv. 9, 15, 31, 39; Θ in vv. 1, 12, 13, 36, 40. Yet Westcott (Smith's *D.B.* I. 397a, ed. 2, 714a) thinks that some of Θ's changes arose from a desire to give consistency to the facts. The change at the end of v. 27, however, is hardly a happy one, καὶ εἶπεν being put immediately after ὁ δράκων, thus suggesting the idea that the latter drew attention to the fact that he was destroyed. The LXX. avoided this.

It is remarkable that Theodoret, in his *Commentary on Daniel*, comments on vv. 1 and 2 of Bel and the Dragon (Θ) only, treating them as the closing verse (14) of chap. xii., and introducing them with the words, οὕτω πληρώσας τὴν ἀποκάλυψιν ἐπήγαγεν ὁ προφήτης· καὶ ὁ βασιλεὺς Ἀστυάγης, κ.τ.λ. This curious fact, combined with that of their omission from the Ο΄, points to some arrangement of the text with which we are not acquainted. Theodoret also refers to these same verses previously, in commenting on chaps. v. 3 and x. 1. Though he says nothing of the rest of Bel and the Dragon, he shews, by his referring in Ep. cxlv. (latter part) to Habakkuk's miraculous flight through the air, that he was well acquainted with the story, and approved of it.

The principal MSS. available are A, B, Q, Γ (vv. 2-4 only), and Δ from v. 21 to 41, which has recently reinforced our somewhat scanty uncial authorities.

The text of A appears to have slightly better Greek (vv. 9, 10, 19, 21, 27); but the form μαχαίρης (occurs in Heb. xi. 34 in A), if not a slip,[67] seems Ionic (Wordsworth's *Greek Gram.* § 16, Obs.), as has been already mentioned ('Authorship,' p. 193), and might perhaps be accounted for by Θ's connection with Ephesus. The substitution of πρός for τῷ, however, in v. 34 seems no improvement, A in this, as in several other instances (vv. 10, 28, 35), agreeing with the Ο΄ reading. Taking, for convenience, B as the norm, we find that A's departures from it are somewhat larger than in the Song of the Three. In v. 7 οὐδὲ πέπωκεν πώποτε is added, as also in Q, to the description of Bel's inability to consume food. In v. 11 δακτύλῳ is curiously substituted by A for δακτυλίῳ; in v. 13 κατεφθόνουν for κατεφρόνουν. Both these are suggestive of carelessness or of error *ex ore dictantis* (Scrivener, *N.T. Criticism*, ed. 2, p. 10). In v. 36 the substitution of χειρός for κορυφῆς is peculiar. The alteration of gender in v. 17, σῶαι for σῶοι in its first occurrence, but not in its second, may come under the head of those "somewhat officious corrections" with which the editors of I. Macc. in the *Camb. Bible for Schools* (p. 48) charge this MS., as likewise perhaps the reading παιδίων for τέκνων in v. 10.

·[67] There is clearly a slip in v. 35 of Δανιήλ for Ἀμβακούμ, and probably·
in v. 11 of δακτύλῳ for δακυλίῳ, indicating some mistakes on the scribe's
part, or errors in his copy.

Q not unfrequently agrees with it in differing from B. It stands alone, however, in reading ναὸν for ἱερὸν in v. 22, and in omitting the last six words of v. 41, perhaps as improbable when coming from Cyrus. Together with A, it contains an additional clause in v. 24, putting words into Cyrus' mouth which connect the two stories together. Γ, having vv. 2-4 only, contains no important variation. Δ (only from v. 21 to v. 41) contains in v. 22 the curious word ἔγδομα instead of ἔκδοτον.

All things considered, the text of both versions may be said to be in as fair condition as in the canonical part of Daniel.

LANGUAGE AND STYLE.

LANGUAGE.

[*See* corresponding title in Susanna.]

The indications of a Semitic original give this fragment, in that respect, a middle place between the other two. Less numerous than in the Song of the Three, they are more so than in the History of Susanna, though this is a shorter piece than that.

The non-discovery by Origen and others of Hebrew originals in their own day by no means goes so far as to prove that such never existed, as Rothstein in Kautzsch (I. 179) truly says.

Since Gaster's discovery of an Aramaic text of the Dragon (not of Bel), the probability of a Semitic rather than a Greek original seems strengthened. But see what Schürer thinks, under the corresponding title in the Song of the Three, as also of the Syriac version at the end of Neubauer's *Tobit*. C.H. Toy, too, in his article in the *Jewish Encyclopædia*, Vol. II, says: "In the present state of knowledge it seems better to reserve opinion as to its antiquity."

Delitzsch, at the end of his *Commentatio de Hab. proph. vita atque ætate* (Lips. 1842), prints in Rabbinic characters a Persian rendering, "ex codice Paris-Reg. judaico-persico," which he says "ex textu hebraico vel aramaico factam esse, ex crebris hebraismis patet" (p. 105). And on pp. 26, 27 he prints the LXX from v. 28 to the end, and adds: "Hæc omnia ad verbum Hebraico vel Aramaico translata esse dictionis simplicitas, structura ac tota indoles clamat atque testatur." But on p. 41 he quotes the opinion of Prof. Solomon Munk, of Paris (*Notice sur Rab. Saadia Gaon*, p. 84), that this Hebrew text, translated into Persian, was itself made by some European Rabbi from the Greek or

Latin Bible. And a similar origin for Gaster's text is now thought far from unlikely.

It may be well here to give a few brief notes on the separate phrases as they occur:

v. 3 Θ. With ἐδαπανῶντο, cf. 'אֲכַלֶּה ב of Deut. xxxii. 23 ("I will spend my arrows upon," etc.). Δαπανάω occurs with ἐν and ἐπί in N.T. Greek, but apparently not with εἰς, nor yet in the canonical O.T. Deissmann, however, attempts to shew that this use of εἰς, instead of 'dativus commodi,' is an Alexandrian idiom (*Bible Studies*, Eng. tr., Edinb. 1900, p. 127). כלא is also used in Aramaic in the same sense in Pahel.

v. 6 O´. The same phrase as the last recurs, inverted: εἰς αὐτὸν δαπανᾶται.

v. 7 O´. Here the accusative after ὀμνύω might be taken as favouring a Greek original, since ἐν for ב would seem natural in a translation of Hebrew or Aramaic.

v. 7 Θ; v. 11 O´, Θ; v. 27 O´. The occurrence of βασιεῦ in these verses suggests a rendering of מַלְכָּא which is used several times in the Aramaic portion of Daniel, while it never occurs in the vocative in the Hebrew portion. This indication, small though it be, inclines of course towards an Aramaic rather than a Hebrew original.

v. 10 O´, Θ. Scholz's suggestion that χωρίς and ἐκτός are translations of לבר is more probable than some of his ideas, for it is rendered by both these words more than once in the Greek O.T.

v. 12 Θ. ὁ ψευδόμενος καθ᾽ ἡμῶν might be a translation of שְׁקָר צָל or צָל.כְּדַב צָל is occasionally rendered by κατά, as in Job xxxiii. 10, in a hostile sense. Liddell and Scott, however, give one example of ψεύδω with κατά, and Arnold an anonymous one in his *Greek Grammar* (1848, p. 265).

v. 13 Θ. Διόλου looks like a translation of תָּמִיד (or תְּדִירָא), as in I. Kings x. 8, where it is so rendered.

v. 14 O´. σφραγισάμενος presents a difficulty here, which may be solved by supposing that חֲתַם had been read by mistake for סְתַם, a kind of error characteristic of the LXX translators. To 'shut' seems more in place here than to 'seal,' which naturally follows later in the verse; shutting first, sealing second, seems the only intelligible order.

vv. 14, 28 Θ; vv. 15, 33 O´. The καὶ ἐγένετο of these verses is suggestive of וַיְהִי in the original.

v. 18 Θ. (Δόλος) οὐδὲ εἷς has an 'ungreek' look, and may have been a rendering of צַד אֶחָד, as in Exod. xiv. 28. (חדא for חזא (חדה) חזה might account for the king's 'rejoicing' in O´ becoming his 'seeing' in Θ.

v. 19 O´, Θ. The reading of ἔδαφος by Θ instead of δόλος by O´ may be accounted for by supposing שקפא to have been substituted for שקרא, as suggested in Hastings' *Dict.*

v. 26 O´, Θ. The use of καί instead of ἵνα, to begin a clause signifying purpose, is very Hebraic.

v. 27 O´, Θ. The ingenious idea of A. Scholz that τὰ σεβάσματα ὑμῶν and οὐ ταῦτα σέβεσηε are renderings of הפחדיכם and הפחדתם respectively, ה in the first case being the article, and in the second merely the interrogative particle, like other conjectures on p. 202 of his *Commentary*, can hardly stand. He appears to have forgotten that the article must not be placed before a noun with a pronominal suffix.[68]

-----

[68] The same writer, on p. 224, spells מאה with a final ם.

-----

v. 28 O´, Θ. ἐπί looks like a translation of צל (*cf.* Sus. 29). In O´ it is used against Daniel, and in Θ against the king.

v. 33 O´. Delitzsch suggests (p. 27) השׁשׁי ויהי ויהי ביום for the beginning of this verse, with much likelihood.

v. 36 Θ. The reading χειρός in A for κορυφῆς may have arisen from קדקדו being corrupted by homœoteleuton into קדו, for which A has read ידו. A. Scholz's notion of explaining this by Isai. xlv. 1 (where δεξιά is used, not χείρ) is unsatisfactory.

v. 40 O´, Θ. The attempt to explain (Marshall in Hastings' *D.B.* art. *Bel and the Dragon*) the 'in medio' of Vulg. v. 39 by a reading בגו for בגב is not very likely, since they do not occur in corresponding clauses.

v. 42 O´. Ἐξήγαγεν is used of the king here in a good sense, in v. 22 in a bad one. This is possibly a rendering of הרציא in the latter case, of הצלה in the former.

The Greek of the writer is hardly such as we should expect, unless he was narrating a story which had reached him from a Hebrew source. The frequency with which verbs occur very early in the construction of sentences is a point in favour of a Semitic original, which does appear to have been dwelt upon, *e.g.* vv. 11, 20 (O´), and 14, 16, 22 (Θ).

It is a matter of considerable nicety to estimate the value of these and similar indications. They are not decisive. They tell with varying force upon varying minds; but they distinctly tend, in the writer's opinion, to increase the probability of the Greek having been grounded upon a Hebrew or an Aramaic form of the story, the likelihood of the latter being slightly the stronger.

In view of the introduction of Habakkuk into the story of the Dragon, Delitzsch's opinion as to the similarity of Daniel's Hebrew to the Hebrew of that prophet (*see* Streane, *Age of Macc.* p. 262) becomes of importance. A. Scholz, too, is of opinion (p. 146) that the Habakkuk title makes for a Hebrew original, because the real prophecy of Habakkuk was undoubtedly Hebrew, and this piece, whether genuine or fictitious, would hardly have been appended in another language.

The LXX version was certainly known to Theodotion, since he copies much of it, yet not quite so largely as in the Song of the Three. But it is evident that he had other documents or traditions to use, of which he freely availed himself; possibly some previous translation other than LXX, as has been suggested under Susanna ('Date and Place,' p. 114). There seems nothing in either Greek recension to imply that the two parts of Bel and the Dragon (separated in Luther's version) are not by the same hand.

It is noteworthy that the word ἔχδοτον, applied to Bel when handed over to Daniel (v. 22, Θ), is used of our Lord in Acts ii. 23, these two being its only Biblical occurrences.

STYLE.

The style is that of simple, clear, and well-told narrative, with very little rhetorical embellishment about it, yet bearing somewhat of a dramatic cast, like much of the canonical book to which it is appended. It is not tedious (though there is much to tell which might have been easily spun out), but is brief and spirited. There is nothing superfluous to the aim of the story.[69]

[69] It is even given in L.C. Cope's *English Composition* (Lond., 1900), as an example of the four essentials of composition, viz. invention, selection, disposition, diction. He also speaks (p. 29) of the "superb workmanship in framing the narrative."

Moreover, the narrative is told in such a way as ever to be a story of captivating interest to the young, being full of movement and interesting incident. The style of the composition is much more in accordance with Syrian than with Alexandrian models. There is nothing of Hellenistic speculation or philosophy, though the subject of idolatry would have lent itself to such treatment (as that of injustice would in Susanna). No figurative or hyperbolic phraseology is employed.

An idea has been revived and maintained that the lions' den episode at the end is a mere adaptation and embellishment of that in Dan. vi.[70] (Churton, 392; Streane, 109, "distortions of O.T. narratives"; J.M. Fuller, S.P.C.K. *Comm. in loc.*). This idea is successfully opposed by Arnald, who (on v. 31) gives three reasons against it, and by Bishop Gray (*Introd. to O.T. in loc.*). Delitzsch (p. 30) calls this section of Θ's version "partem dignissimam." Attempts to prove the falsity of this martyrdom, if such it may be called, by first assuming the identity of these two events, treating the latter as an ornamental exaggeration of the former, and then pointing out what are taken for irreconcileable discrepancies, are beside the mark. Nor does the supposition that the one night in the den (of Dan. vi.) was increased to six, nor that the detail of withholding the lions' usual food to sharpen their appetites (in Θ only), were added for the purpose of heightening the effect, carry much weight. The omission of Daniel's speech, with the detail[71] of the angel closing the lions' mouths (vv. 21, 22), tells in the opposite direction. It is no more necessary to reckon these two den episodes as one event than our Lord's feeding of the four and five thousand, or his healing of the centurion's servant and the nobleman's son.

[70] Bar Hebræus (*op. cit.*, p. 27), gives this as a reason why some would not receive Bel and the Dragon.

[71] Not in O'.

RELIGIOUS AND SOCIAL STATE.

RELIGIOUS.

A religious feeling, strong though misdirected, evidently existed both in king and people, involving considerable expenditure on objects and places of worship. It was not as to the propriety of worship in itself, but of the object towards which it ought to be directed, that the controversy arose.

Two sorts of worship were in vogue:—

(a) *Bel-worship.* As to the practice of this in Babylon no question appears to be raised; he was the supreme god and guardian of Babylon. The representation of Cyrus as a worshipper of Bel agrees with the account of himself in the Annals of Nabu-nahid, cited by Ball on v. 4; and Sayce (*Temple Bible*, Tobit, p. 95) notes that the cuneiform monuments have shewn that Cyrus was politic enough to conform to the religion of his Babylonian subjects.

The unabashed effrontery of the idol-priests (vv. 11, 12) is very characteristic. See, however, Blakesley's note on Herodot. VIII. 41.

(b) *Dragon-worship.* This is not otherwise known to have existed in Babylonia, but snake-worship, which may be the same, is asserted by J.T. Marshall (end of art. *Bel and the Dragon*, Hastings' *D.B.*). In support of this it is noteworthy that ὁ δράκων is identified with ὁ ὄφις in Rev. xii. 9, and that נָחָשׁ and תַּנִּין seem identified in Ex. iv. 3 and vii. 9. A. Kamphausen, in the *Encycl. Bibl.*, thinks that "Günkel has conclusively shewn that the primeval Babylonian myth of the conquest of the chaos-monster or the great dragon Tiamat by the god Marduk lies at the root." So J.M. Fuller, in the S.P.C.K. *Comm.*, says that "in Babylonian inscriptions dealing with the fall, a dragon, generally female, appears." Daniel plans his scheme in accordance with the dragon's known voracity (Jer. li. 34). The προσεκύνησαν τὸν δράκοντα of Rev. xiii. 4 may have been suggested by the dragon-worship here; ἐσέβοντο is used in v. 23, προσκύνησον (with dat.) in v. 24 (both versions).

Daniel set himself, in reply to the king, who suggested to him the propriety of Bel-worship, to detach the Babylonians from these superstitious follies, to interpret God's will in the matter, and to free them from the service of idols. Yet his own name, 'Belteshazzar,' may have implied[72] Bel's existence; still, even if it was so, we must remember that it was not self-assumed, but given by the chief eunuch. The king's question shews that he misunderstood Daniel's character. It is noticeable, as a link of connection between the two parts of the story, that Daniel attacks the former superstition, Bel, by disproving the belief in the god's powers of eating; and the latter, the Dragon, by destroying the supposed divinity by means of what he ate.

[72] See note to 'For Whom and with What Object' p. 196.

As described in the Greek, Daniel's method of destroying the Dragon appears quite inadequate to effect his purpose. The ingredients named as composing the ball do not seem capable of achieving the result which followed. But in Gaster's Aramaic a different light is thrown upon the matter; for the ball is merely used as a vehicle to conceal sharp teeth embedded in it, so that the Dragon might swallow them unawares, and sustain internally a fatal laceration. If this be accepted as correct, Sir Thomas Browne's discussion, as to how such unlikely ingredients might bring about a death of the kind described, is naturally set aside. S. Wilkin, however, in his edition of Browne's *Works*, 1835 (Vol. II. p. 337), does not treat Sir T. Browne's discussion as a serious one; but in this view all will not concur. Schürer, in Hauck's *Dict.* (I. 639), writes of the Dragon as having been slain "mit unverdaulichen Kitchen"; and Toy, in the *Jewish Encyclopædia*, regards "the iron comb insertion as a natural embellishment." It is, however, not at all out of keeping with Daniel's clever devices for the detection of error, and looks like a practicable plan. And Josippon, quoted by Heppner, *op. cit.* p. 33, gives a similar account of the Dragon's destruction, והחרוצים קרני הברזל.

The consequence of the prophet's triumph in each case appears to have been that the king was convinced of the vanity of idols much more than his people. And as Daniel's demonstrations were not, so far as we see, made before the general public, this is what might have been expected. A similar conviction on Nebuchadnezzar's part, without any spontaneous assent of his people, may be noticed in Dan. iii. 28-30, vi. 25-28. A lack of popular adhesion to the king's change of mind would sufficiently account for the early restoration of Bel's temple (*see* 'Chronology,' p. 225).

In v. 21 the LXX states that it was Daniel who shewed the king the privy doors. This, on the whole, has more *vraisemblance* than the idea of Theodotion, who states that it was the priests who undertook the task. Ball suggests that they did so because they were "in fear of their lives"; but if so, this plan of saving them, by making a clean breast of the matter, was unsuccessful.

Another religious feature shews itself in v. 28, viz. the scorn in which the Babylonian zealots held the Jewish religion. It would evidently have been regarded as a degradation for the king to become a Jew, and social would probably here combine with religious grounds in giving force to this feeling. Compare Pilate's contempt of such an idea with regard to himself, as expressed in St. John xviii. 35. Grotius proposed a translation which inverted the phrase in such a way as to make it apply to Daniel: "A Jew has become king." This, however, is not natural in the Greek, has no countenance lent to it by the Aramaic text, and is clearly opposed by the Syriac marginal title as given in Swete's manual LXX, "tit. adpinx. ut vid. περι του βασιλεως λεγουσι ως γεγονεν Ιουδαιος, Syr^mg." Cajetanus Bugati also (*Daniel*, Milan, 1788, p. 162) thinks Grotius wrong.[73] For a similarly imagined instance of a king embracing Judaism, *cf.* II. Macc. ix. 17, headed by A.V., "Antiochus promiseth to become a Jew," on which Rawlinson notes, "it is extremely improbable that Epiphanes ever expressed any such intention," an opinion in which most will agree.

[73] Compare the Aramaic of the passage, given under 'Chronology,' p. 229.

The withholding of food, in order to sharpen the lions' appetites (v. 32), shews a spirit similar to that which directed the sevenfold heating of the furnace in chap. iii. The numbers in vv. 2, 10, etc., are quite in keeping with Daniel's use of symbolic numeration for purposes of religious teaching; and the zeal displayed against idolatry is characteristic of the Jewish captivity, as depicted in the canonical book which bears his name. These three points, therefore, so far as they go, tell in favour of the religious unity of the whole.

SOCIAL.

Daniel appears on the same terms of intimacy with royalty as in the canonical book, and speaks his mind a little more freely and intimately perhaps, as becomes his added years and experience. He still acts as a divine messenger to a heathen king, and he successfully unmasks his fallacy of judging by appearances in the matter of Bel's food. His laughter in vv. 7,19, may have been amusement at the king's simplicity or at the priests' cunning, the king's wrath in vv. 8, 21, being compatible with either. But this laughter of v. 7 only appears in Θ's version. As in Susanna, he stands as the willing exposer of fraud, intellectually acute as well as morally upright.

v. 29 Θ has been objected to by Ball and by Zöckler as an unlikely mode of address by the conquered Babylonians to Cyrus their conqueror. Probably some tumultous rising took place, which the king, a true oriental monarch, pacified at the expense of Daniel. On such outbreaks courtly politeness often vanishes, and the tyrant is subject to tyranny. Such an occurrence agrees with Habakkuk's description of the Chaldees as "bitter and hasty" (i. 6), and 'senseless' and 'absurd' are scarcely the terms to apply to it.

The slaughter of the priests (vv. 22, 28) is quite in accordance with the practice as shewn in the canonical chapters ii. and vi.[74]; also the destruction of false accusers (v. 42) with vi. 25; so also the keeping of lions by the king; and so, too, the method of double sealing (v. 11 O´, 14 Θ; vi. 17). That παιδάρια should be under the command of Daniel (v. 14 Θ and Syr.) is what would be likely for one in his position. The term is used of himself in Sus. 45 Θ as a page of superior rank. The idea of an image being made of more materials than one (v. 7) is paralleled in ii. 32, 33.

[74] On the propriety of such a sentence, accordant with Babylonian ideas of justice, see Mozley, *Ruling O.T. Ideas,* 1878, pp. 88, 95, 99.

Cyrus' cowardice in giving up Daniel to the threatening mob is very like Pilate's in delivering up Christ (St. Matt, xxvii. 26, St. John xix. 16). Παραδίδωμι is used in each case (v. 29 Θ, 30 Θ and O´). Similar, too, is Nebuchadnezzar's conduct with Daniel, and that of Herod Antipas with St. John Baptist. Despotic rulers are often frightened by popular clamour. But Cyrus, however weak in yielding, appears at the close of the story in a less odious light than Pilate.

As in Susanna, there is no indication of rabbinism in the legal, religious, or social standpoints of the story.

THEOLOGY.

The whole piece makes a mock at idolatry[75] with a view of turning men from false worships to that of the living God. Indeed the end of v. 5 seems an echo of Gen. i. 1. Jehovah's power to vindicate Himself and His servants is of course also exhibited, and this in contrast to the idols, who make no resistance to their overthrow.

[75] "More withering sarcasm could scarcely be poured on heathenism· than in the apocryphal story of Bel and the Dragon" (Edersheim, *Life and* *Times of Messiah*, 1886, I. 31). Daniel's laugh in v. 7 accords with Jeremiah's view of idols (X. 15). Other coincidences with Jeremiah may be noted in 1. 2, li. 44 of that prophet.

He is represented as Sole Sovereign, the only God worthy of worship, with full power to deliver by wonderful providence His faithful people, who make their acknowledgments to Him. However far they may be scattered, His eye is still upon them; He forsakes not those who seek and love Him (v. 38).

vv. 3, 4, 14 are quoted by Irenæus (IV. ix. 1) to prove that the one living God was the God worshipped by the prophets, as "the God of the living." Even the heathen king is forced to confess that He is great and unique, and (in Vulg. only, v. 42) calls Him Saviour, and desires the whole world to worship Him.

It is noteworthy that the king is represented as the party complaining in the first instance; it is his question (v. 4) which draws forth from Daniel his practical proof of the vanity of idols, inanimate or animate, culminating in the triumphant exclamation at the end of v. 27. And thus the imposture of idol-worship is revealed, as well as the value of devotion to the true Lord of all, by a process commenced in the opposite interest.

Daniel resists the king's invitation to worship Bel, which might have led him under the ban of Deut. xviii. 20 (end) as "speaking in the name of other gods." False theological opinions are corrected by Daniel, who not only dissuades from idol-worship, but persuades to that of the true deity. Hence the beautiful appropriateness of τοὺς ἀγαπῶντάς σε (v. 38) instead of τοὺς ἐλπίζοντας ἐπ' αὐτὸν in the corresponding point of delivery in Sus. 60 Θ. For Daniel was fighting for God, while Susanna was defending herself. The one was an active plaintiff for God, the other a passive defendant of herself. Thus Love in Daniel's case, Hope in Susanna's, has its own special appropriateness.

In v. 5 Daniel claims God to be τὸν ζῶντα θεόν, but Cyrus claims for Bel to be only ζῶν θεός; in v. 24 Cyrus makes the same claim for the Dragon, and then in v. 25 Daniel makes only a like claim for God (anarthrous), for Daniel takes here the words out of Cyrus' mouth; in the former instance it was *vice versâ.* The same phrases are used by Darius in vi. 20, 26 Θ. Thus the prophet makes a more exclusive claim for the divinity of his God. In v. 6 a contrast is afforded with what is said of God in Ps. xvi. 2 (P.B. aft. Vulg. and LXX), as the Creator who still retains power over living beings.

As in the canonical Dan. vi. 22 (and in the other additions thereto), so here an angel intervenes on behalf of the right, rescuing God's persecuted prophet. A man is employed in each case also to carry out the miraculous purposes of God. Further, compare the angel helping Daniel, after conflict with the Dragon, with Rev. xii. 7, 8.

The sudden transportation of Habakkuk (v. 36) is parallelled by that of St. Philip in Acts viii. 39 by the "Spirit of the Lord." Ezek. viii. 3, which is printed as a parallel in the margin of A.V. at iii. 12, 14 of that book, may also be compared,[76] as well as I. Kings xviii. 12 and St. Matt. iv. I. For the latter part of this verse (36), barely intelligible in the Greek, Gaster's Aramaic gives an excellent sense.

[76] Ezekiel is transported in the opposite direction, and both prophets went unwillingly (Trapp). Both, too, were concerned in suppression of idolatry.

There does not seem to be any undue love of the marvellous or straining to bring it into prominence. Both the statue and the Dragon are destroyed by ordinary means; and their false position in the imagination of the people is unmasked without any resort to the miraculous.[77] This element does not enter into the story till the rescue of the persecuted Daniel, who has been so zealous for the honour of his God.

[77] The destruction of the Dragon, by means which in A.V. and the Greek appear inadequate, does not come under this head, since the Aramaic explains it by iron teeth concealed in the ball (v. 27), an intelligible and practical device.

Though, with its two companion pieces, it has been cavilled at (not to reckon Africanus' enquiries) from the time of the Jewish teacher whom Jerome tells us of in his preface to Daniel, yet even the most contemptuous deprecators of the 'Additions' can find little seriously to condemn in the theology of this story.[78] Considering the strong desire which has existed in some quarters to charge these apocryphal books with grievous doctrinal error, this fact says much. The knowledge of God and of divine things is what would be probable at the time it represents, and is not incongruous with the book to which it is appended, nor with its fellow-appendices. This speaks well for its excellence and its consistency.

CHRONOLOGY.

The principal chronological points, concerning which difficulties have been felt, arise: (A) in vv. 1, 2, concerning Astyages, Cyrus, and Daniel; (B) in v. 22, as to the destruction of Bel's temple; and (C) in v. 33, as to Habakkuk being a contemporary of Daniel.

In connection with A, it is remarkable that v. 1 forms in the Vulgate the last verse of the preceding chapter, *i.e.* the last verse of Susanna. This arrangement may have been made from chronological reasons, possibly to escape an apparent difficulty; and in the LXX the verse is wanting altogether. Either plan, the attachment of the verse to Susanna, or its entire omission, has the effect of leaving the king in this piece nameless, and so solves the imagined difficulty of Cyrus and Daniel acting together as represented.

The text commented on by Theodoret offers the same solution in another form, viz. by transferring v. 1 to the end of chap, xii., and so concluding the book. He thus introduces it: Οὕτω πληρώσας τὴν ἀποκάλυψιν ἐπήγαγεν ὁ προφήτης καὶ ὁ βασιλεὺς Ἀστυάγης, κ.τ.λ. Theodoret comments no further on Bel and the Dragon, though his remarks in other parts of the commentary shew that he favourably regarded it. See his observations on v. 31, x. 1.

The disappearance in one case, and the displacements in the others of this verse, evidently point to some uncertainty in early times as to its right connection. But the difficulties raised as to this verse even where it stands are not so serious as was once thought. As Ball says *in loc.*, "The cuneiform records have thrown unexpected light on difficulties which were the despair of bygone generations of scholars," and quotes one which makes Astyages the captive of Cyrus. J.H. Blunt attempts to shew, not very satisfactorily, that the king of v. 2 was Darius. A note in Husenbeth's Douay version, still less so, quietly says "Astyages, or Darius"!

It has also been suggested, with regard to this and difficulty C, that another Daniel is here intended, to be identified with the Daniel of Ezra viii. 2 (Bissell).

The second difficulty, B, is raised by the asserted destruction of Bel's temple in v. 22. Now this is said not to have been destroyed till Xerxes' return from Greece in 479. Even then Herodotus (I. 183) merely says that he 'took' (ἔλαβε) a golden statue, and slew the protesting priest; Strabo, on hearsay,

(XVI. 1) and Arrian (*Exp. Alex.* VII. 17), however, assert its destruction. But this forms a small obstacle, unduly magnified. Supposing Bel's temple to have been destroyed, as v. 22 narrates, it is far from improbable that another temple may have been raised before Xerxes' arrival. The people were evidently attached to Bel's worship, as v. 28 shews, notwithstanding the conviction of their king as to the truth of Daniel's God. It is noticeable that the LXX has no mention of the temple's, but only of the idol's, destruction; and that Θ, according to the manuscript Q, has not ἱερόν but ναόν in v. 22.

A. Scholz entertains the strange opinion that this and other historic difficulties were purposely introduced by the writer: "Der Verfasser unserer Erzählung kennt sichtlich die Verhältnisse in Babylon, und hat seine Darstellung so eingerichtet, dass es einfach unmöglich ist, sie geschichtlich zu verstehen" (p. 219). But this is a desperate expedient to support his view of the whole story being intended for a 'vision,' and it would be hard to find any parallel to such a proceeding on the part of the sacred writers.[79]

[79] The phrase applied to the Additions in the *Introd. to Daniel* in the *Speaker's Comm.* (p. 216a), דברי פיוטין if we take פיוט to mean 'poet,' would fall in with this view. J.M. Fuller does not make quite clear his source for this phrase.

So far as Babylon is concerned, there is no indication of anything but a time of peace, which is quite in accordance with the supposed period of the narrative.

There is perhaps more difficulty, C, in making Habakkuk than in making Cyrus, a contemporary of the grown-up Daniel. Indeed, with the earlier date formerly assigned to Habakkuk, the difficulty seemed all but insuperable, except by postulating two Habakkuks or two Daniels. And, much as it may lack *vraisemblance*, either of those suppositions is of course within the bounds of possibility. So Trapp notes, rather sneeringly, on Hab. i. 1: "Those apocryphal Additions to Daniel, which either are false, or there were two Habakkuks"; and J.H. Blunt, more seriously, to a similar effect on Hab. i. 1 and Bel 33. Josippon ben Gorion (I. 7) joins the whole story with the canonical history, but, as given by Delitzsch (*op. cit.* p. 40), transposes, presumably from chronological motives, the den incident to the beginning of the story, "in ordine chronologico iudaicæ traditioni de Habacuci ætate se accommodantem." Josippon, around whom considerable obscurity hangs, is dated as of the eighth or ninth century in the *Biog. Univ.* art. *Gorionides*, Paris, 1857; but in Hastings' *D.B.* art *Bel and the Dragon*, p. 267b, c. A.D. 940 is given as his time.

Habakkuk's prophecy is now dated as late as 600 (Driver in Hastings' *D.B.* art. *Habakkuk*; Kirkpatrick in Smith's *D.B².* art. *Habakkuk*, 1256b, says "not later than the sixth year of Jehoiakim"); and if Habakkuk prophesied in his youth, our story is not an impossible one. So Cornelius Jansen (*Analecta*, p. 154), "Quapropter nihil obstabit quo minus idem Habacuc iam senex prandium in Babylonem detulerit," and he quotes a tradition of Isidore Hispalensis (*de vit. Proph.*) that Habakkuk lived to see the return from the Captivity, and two years after. Rosenmüller, quoted in a note on Hab. i. 1 by Maurer (neither of whom were too partial to traditional views), thinks that the time of Habakkuk is consistent with the "vetus fama in apocryphis Danielis additamentis." He even places chap. iii. of Habakkuk under Zedekiah, though with this Maurer does not agree (*cf.* Henderson, *Min. Proph., Introd. to Hab.*).

Jamieson, Brown, and Faussett in their Commentary, *Introd. to Hab.* (1869), by no means inclined to favour the Apocrypha, say that Bel and the Dragon agrees with the notion of Habakkuk prophesying in Jehoiakim's reign.

G.A. Smith, however, in his *Book of the Twelve Prophets*, 1900, II. 130, contents himself with calling it "an extraordinary story of Habakkuk's miraculous carriage of food to Daniel in the lions' den, soon after Cyrus had taken Babylon." But A.C. Jennings, in Bishop Ellicott's *Comm. for English Readers, Introd. to Hab.*, pp. 523-5, says: "The story, worthless in itself, nevertheless, indirectly confirms the theory of date which we have accepted below" in these words, "Habakkuk's prophecy dates from the reign of Jehoiakim, not more than five years at most before the battle of Carchemish—how much nearer that great event it is impossible to say." Dean Farrar also curiously observes, "Habakkuk's appearance in apocryphal legend (vv. 33-39) shews the impression he had made on the mind of his people, and perhaps indicates his date as a contemporary of Daniel." (*Minor Prophets* in 'Men of the Bible' series, n.d., p. 160).

Another instance of belief in the contemporaneity of Daniel and Habakkuk is afforded by Raymund Martini (*c.* 1250) in his *Pugio fidei* (Paris, 1651, p. 740): "Habacuc vero Prophetam fuisse contemporaneum Danieli inde colligitur ubi in Bereschit Rabba hoc modo scribitur de Joseph," he says before quoting a long passage from the B.R. on Gen. xxxvii. 24. This passage is none other than a portion of Bel and the Dragon in Chaldee, and is headed without reserve as בדניאל. It proceeds with v. 28 to the end: לכא לביל תבד ולתנינא קטל ואתהפכו צליו ואמרין חד לחד יהודאה הוא ליה ואיתכנשו בבלאי צל מלכא. Then follows a Latin translation, after which Martini adds "Hucusque traditio," and, after quoting Hab. i. 6, finishes his work.

Martini's good faith in quotation is defended by Neubauer in his Chaldee Tobit (Oxf, 1888, xviii. to xxiv.). He also identifies the Breshith Rabbah quoted with the Midrash Rabbah de Rabbah. The real Breshith is probably as early as the 4th century; but neither in the Venice edition of 1566, nor the

Leipzig one of 1864, is the passage to be found under Gen. xxxvii. *Cf.* Payne-Smith's note, as to Martini's quotations, in *Pearson on the Creed*, Oxf. 1870, p. 306, where it is shewn that by Breshith Rabbah the book by Moses Haddarshan (of the 11th century) is sometimes meant. Etheridge states that only fragments of this book are extant (p. 406). Delitzsch (*de Habacuci Proph. vita atque ætate*, Lips. 1842, p. 34) also defends Martini's sincerity, and says "Non dubito fore, ut fragmentum a Raymundo nobiscum communicatum aliquando in antiquis Genesis Rabba Codd., qui sane rarissimi sunt, inveniatur."

The fact incidentally brought out in the story that Habakkuk was not engaged in reaping, but was occupied in taking out food for the reapers, fits in well with the idea of his advanced age. Such a task might well be undertaken by one who was no longer strong enough for field labour.[80]

[80] Sozomen, *H.E.* vii. 29, says that Habakkuk's tomb was found at Keilah, κελὰ, ἡ πρὶν κείλα... καθ᾽ ἥν ὁ Ἀβακοὺμ (*sic*) εὑρέθη. Now Keilah is mentioned in I Sam. xxiii. 1 as having threshing-floors worth robbing, and so presumably lay in a corn-growing district.

All these difficulties would, on other grounds, be deprived of much of their importance by the theory of A. Scholz, if that could be accepted as true. He regards the entire book of Daniel, including of course the Additions, as a series of apocalyptic visions (p. 201). This he considers as the earliest explanation, supported by the heading ὅραις to each chapter of Daniel in A and some other MSS. But while removing one set of difficulties, this theory introduces others of a character at least as serious; and it is by no means easy to convince oneself that there is an "apocalyptic" tone about this or the other Additions. This remarkable theory cuts, rather than unties, such knots as are above noted, and carries with it to most minds a strange and improbable air.

CANONICITY.

What is said as to Susanna on this point holds almost entirely good here. Both pieces have been called in question on nearly the same ground, and have stood or fallen together. Possibly this one presents rather more difficulty in some of its details.

It is often included in Scripture lists under the title Daniel;[81] and is often quoted in the same manner, *e.g.* by St. Cyprian, *ad Fortunatum*, § 11, "Daniel, Deo devotus & sancto spiritu plenus exclamat et dicit," v. 4. The quotations given under 'Early Christian Literature and Art' will shew how strong a hold this story had in many quarters, and what use was made of it.

Delitzech thought it likely, though not certain, that the βιβλία mentioned by Josephus (*Ant.* x. 11. 7) as left by Daniel refer to the Additions as portions of the canonical book (*De Hab. vita*, etc., Lips. 1842, p. 25).

Pseudo-Athanasius, in his *Synops. S.S.*, mentions the story at the end of Section 41 as included in Daniel, but he does *not* name it at the close of the *Synopsis* as being outside the canonical books, as he does in the case of Susanna. The writer of *De Mirabilibus Script. Sacr.*, often attached to St. Augustine's works (Migne, *Patr. lat.* XXXV.; Benedict, ed. appx. to Vol. III.), expressly declares against its canonicity. This treatise is thought to have been composed in England or Ireland in the 7th or 8th century (Loisy, *O.T.* p. 154).

The hesitation of the earlier Church, however, found no counterpart in the canonizing decree of the Council of Trent; while, on the other hand, Protestant opinion has run almost entirely against canonicity. Diametrically opposite views are steadily maintained by authorities on both sides; although among English-speaking Protestants there is perhaps a decrease in the contempt with which this story was once treated.

Among the Syriac-using Christians of the Malabar coast, Bel and the Dragon, with the other additions, is reckoned as "part and parcel of the book of Daniel" (Letter to present writer of Aug. 8, 1902, from Rev. F.V.J. Givargese, Principal of Mar Dionysius Seminary, Kottayam). Bar-Hebræus, too, comments on it, but says at the head of his remarks that "some do not receive this story" (*op. cit.* p. 27).

The many, resemblances and coincidences between this and the canonical book pointed out under other heads ('Language and Style,' 'Religious and Social State,' etc.) of course tell, so far as they go, in its favour.

Schrader (Schenkel's *Bibel Lex.* 1869, art. *Habak.* p. 556) classes Bel and the Dragon with pseudo-Epiphanius' and Rabbinic legends of the same tale, as "reine Fabeln und Legenden zu erkennen." This seems too positive an opinion of their untrustworthiness. It is agreed with, however, by Orelli (*Introd.to Hab.*, Clarke's Transl.), who styles Bel and the Dragon, or at least the Habakkuk incident in it, "an idle story." A.B. Davidson also (*Encyclop. Brit.* ed. 9, II. 181) writes of it as being "completely fabulous;" and Ewald speaks of the episode of Habakkuk as an example of an unhistoric spirit, growing rapidly and dangerously (v. 487).

Cloquet's plea that non-canonicity is 'proved' (*XXXIX Arts.* 1885, pp. 112, 113) by six days being named here, and one day in the canonical book, as the length of Daniel's incarceration in the den, is beside the mark. It assumes for controversial purposes that the two passages must refer to the same event.

This writer also speaks generally (p. 115) of Bel and the Dragon's "direct contradictions of Scripture." Such strictures are only worth noticing as specimens of many instances in which *possible* discrepancies between canonical and uncanonical books are treated by a particular class of writers as *certain*, in the hope of depreciating the latter. These are sometimes attacked with extreme violence as full of fables, superstitions, and impieties— apocryphal in the worst sense. But they deserve to be saved from this unmerited contempt, indulged in usually for polemical purposes, and only rendered possible by an insufficient study of the works themselves and the many admirable points which they contain.

Our own Church indulges in no rash or sweeping assertions, but follows the golden mean. She states in Art. VI. her present practical view of this and the other Additions in common with the rest of the Apocrypha. While not making any special doctrine to turn upon an apocryphal text, she directs the perusal of this, with the other books of its class, for purposes of practical edification. In singularly guarded and cautious terms she is careful not to commit herself to anything more than a statement of her authorized practice. Thus she has not closed the door, as the Council of Trent is supposed to have done,[82] against the entry of fresh knowledge, with its corresponding changes of view or modifications of usage.

[82] Cf. *Revue biblique internationale* (Dominican) Paris, Jan. 1901, p. 149, "L'église romaine s'est prononcée dès ce moment, et *si elle ne pas dès lors impose sa solution comme définitive et irréformable*, elle ne s'en est du moins jamais écartée et c'est cette solution qui explique l'unanimité pratique de l'Église latine, où les doutes n'étaient plus que le reflet érudit d'anciennes controverses." See also Sanday on *Inspiration*, Note B. to Lect. V. "The Use of the term Deutero-canonical in the Roman Church."

EARLY CHRISTIAN LITERATURE AND ART

LITERATURE.

The following examples from primitive Christian writings bear more or less directly upon this book.

NEW TESTAMENT. Compare B.V.M.'s words in St. Luke i. 38 with Daniel's at the end of v. 9, Θ. With John xviii. 35 compare Bel 38, O´ and Θ, as to a Gentile being taken for a Jew. Moreover the phrase τὰ σεβάσματα ὑμῶν in Acts xvii. 23 is very like a reminiscence of Bel 27, Θ, end. But A. Scholz's idea that our Lord's words in John x. 9 are based on vv. 3, 6, 13 has little likelihood: "gegensätzlich so nahe verwandt, dass in den Evangelium darauf Bezug genommen sein könnte" (note on v. 13).

IRENÆUS (†200) in IV. ix. 1 quotes vv. 4, 5, 24, as coming from Daniel, apparently without the smallest misgiving. His quotations accord with Θ as against O´, v. 4 being the same in both. As Schürer says in Hauck's *Encyclopædia* (I. 640): "Irenäus benuzt die Uebersetzung des Theodotion und so alle Folgenden." But see under *Cyprian*.

CLEMENT OF ALEXANDRIA (†220) refers, *Strom*. I. 21 (middle, ed. Potter, Oxf. 1715), among a chain of historic events, to the closing scene in this piece: τότε διὰ δράκντα Δανιὴλ εἰς λάκκον λεόντων βληθεὶς, ὑπὸ Ἀμβακοὺβ[83] προνοίᾳ θεῦ τραφεὶς, ἑβδομαῖος ἀνασώζεται.

[83] So spelt in Migne in this instance, though elsewhere with final μ. A misprint may he suspected.

TERTULLIAN (†240). In *de Jejun*. VII. (end) reference is made to vv. 35-39; and in IX. the story is again mentioned. In *de Oratione*, 29, he quotes vv. 33, 34, seemingly with full acceptance. In *de Idol*. XIX. he says that "Daniel nec Belum nec draconem colere."

ORIGEN (†254). Besides the question dealt with in his controversy with Julius Africanus, Origen in the Fragment of his *Strom*, bk. X. expounds Bel. He also quotes it in his *Exhort, ad martyrium*, § 33.

CYPRIAN (†258) in *ad Fortunatum*, 11, quotes v. 5, apparently following a translation of the O´, and not of Θ's, text. The same verse is again quoted by him in *Ep*. lviii. 5 in exactly the same words. It is curious that both passages are preceded, in the same sections, by a quotation of Dan. iii. 16-18, apparently based on Θ's version. In the case of v. 5 in *Ep*. lviii. there is a slight variation in the readings of some MSS. as given by Hartel. *Cf*. Prof. Swete's *Introd*. 1902, p. 47.

PSEUDO-CYPRIAN (3rd century?) gives parts of vv. 37, 38, in *Oratio* II. 2, following O´ a little more closely than Θ.

PASSING OF MARY (3rd or 4th century, *see D.C.B., Mary*, 1142b). In the First Latin form vv. 33-39 are clearly referred to.

ATHANASIUS (†373) in his *Discourse against Arians*, II. 8, quotes v. 5 as words of Daniel, which he also refers to in III. 30.

EPHREM SYRUS (†378). In the hymn *de Jejunio* there is, according to T.J. Lamy (Mechlin, 1886), a reference to Bel and the Dragon, "cum Daniel jejunavit."

GREGORY NAZIANZEN (†390) in his poetical *Præcepta ad Virgines* has the line, speaking of Daniel, ἀερίην δ᾽ ἐνὶ χρσὶν ἐδέξατο δαῖτα προφήτου.

AMBROSE (†397), in his Commentary in *Ep. ad Rom. I. 23*, writes, "Coluerunt et serpentem draconem quem occidit Daniel, homo dei" (Basel, 1527, IV. p. 768).

CHRYSOSTOM (†407), *In Danielem*, cap. XIII. (XIV.) comments on Bel and the Dragon as part of the book, seemingly without reserve or alteration of tone.

PRUDENTIUS (†410), in his *Cathemerinon*, IV., has several verses on the den episode, of which this is one:

"Cernit forte procul dapes ineuntas
Quas messoribus Habakkuk propheta
Agresti bonus exhibebat arte."

JEROME (†420), though excluding this and the other Additions from the canon, according to what he writes in his preface to Daniel, "veru anteposito easque jugulante subjecimus," retains it in his Bible. In his *Onomasticon de Nominibus Hebraicis* he includes under Daniel, Astyages, Bel, Ambacum, without distinction from the rest of the names in Daniel. But for this last work he was chiefly indebted to Eusebius, Πετὶ τῶν οπικῶν ὀνομάτων. (*D.C.B.* II. 336a).

HESYCHIUS OF JERUSALEM (†438), in his Στιχηρὸν on the XII prophets, says of Habakkuk that, whether he was the same Habakkuk as an angel carried to Babylon, εἰπεῖν τὸ σαφὲς οὐκ ἔχω.

THEODORET(†457), towards the close of *Ep.* CXLV., quotes v. 36 with clear belief in the miracle. He also comments on vv. 1, 2 as if forming v. 14 of Dan. xii.; and then ceases.

We see, then, that the more than respectful references to this piece in the writers of ancient Christendom, if not quite so frequent as the citations of the Song and of Susanna, are still numerous and clear.

ART.

This apocryphal tract has afforded two fairly popular subjects for artistic illustration, viz., Daniel destroying the dragon, and Daniel and Habakkuk in the lions' den.

Daniel destroying the Dragon is a subject represented on glass from the catacombs (*D.C.A.* art. *Glass*, p. 733a). Garrucci (*Vetri*, XIII. 13) has a glass vessel in which Christ is represented with Daniel, who is giving cakes to the dragon (*D.C.A. Jesus Christ, Representations of,* p. 877b). In *Paganism in Christian Art* in the same Dictionary (p. 1535a), it is said, "Hercules feeding the fabled dragon with cakes of poppy-seed appears to have furnished the motive for the representation of the apocryphal story of Daniel killing the dragon at

Babylon." Presumably this means the dragon Ladon in the garden of the Hesperides. But the connection between the two dragon episodes of Hercules and Daniel seems a little difficult to establish by indisputable evidence.

In Walter Lowrie's *Christian Art and Archæology* (Lond. and New York, 1901, p. 363) is a woodcut of a fragment of gold glass, with Daniel slaying the Dragon. This is correctly described on p. 209, but is wrongly entitled under the figure itself, as 'Daniel slaying Bel.' The picture is said to be taken from Garrucci, *Storia dell' Arte*, but no further reference is given. On p. 365 of Lowrie's book is a smaller scene of the same in glass, again with an erroneous description on p. xxi. as "Daniel and Bel." No dates are suggested for the above pieces of glass, but they appear to be very ancient.

In the Vatican cemetery a representation of Daniel's destruction of the dragon has been found on a sarcophagus; nor is this a solitary instance. (*See O.T. in Art, D.C.A.* p. 1459a.) And on the south side of the Angel Choir in Lincoln Minster, among a series of sculptures in the spandrils of the triforium arches, occurs a figure, described by Cockerell, the architect, as that of the "Angel of Daniel," with a monster under his feet, deemed to be "the old Dragon " (Archæol. Institute's *Memoirs of Lincoln*, Lond. 1850, p. 222).

Habakkuk with the loaves often appears in representations of the lions' den (*O.T. in Art*, 1459a). In fact there is reason to think that this apocryphal scene was at least as frequently represented as the corresponding canonical one; *e.g.* on a sarcophagus at Rome figured in the frontispiece to Burgon's *Letters from Rome*, thought by him to be of about the 5th century (p. 244). There is also a woodcut of this in *D.C.A.* art. *Sculpture*, p. 1868. A sarcophagus of the 4th century also, like Burgon's, in the Lateran Museum (though not, it would seem, identical) is mentioned in W. Lowrie's *Art and Archæology*, p. 260, as carved with the same subject of Daniel and Habakkuk.

In Bohn's edition of Didron's *Christian Iconography* (Lond. 1886, II. 210) there is a woodcut of a miniature in the *Speculum hum. salv.* (*circ.* 1350), in the library of Lord Coleridge, portraying Daniel among the lions. The appearance of Habakkuk guided by the angel in the background, carrying food, identifies the scene with Bel and the Dragon, and not with the history of Dan. vi. Even in representations of this, the canonical den-scene, it is noteworthy how often Daniel is shown in a sitting posture, although all mention of this is confined to v. 40 of the apocryphal story.

It is a little remarkable that Daniel's dramatic disclosure of the priests' trick (v. 21) has not, so far as the writer is aware, commended itself to artists. The ash-strewn floor of Bel's temple, the tell-tale footmarks, and the emotions of exultation and surprise on the face of Daniel and the King respectively, with a possible introduction of the detected impostors at the side, might make, in capable hands, a very effective picture.

"EXAMPLE OF LIFE AND INSTRUCTION OF MANNERS."

The whole story, in addition to proving the vanity of idols, shews how God watches over the fate of those who bravely discharge his work; while idolaters and persecutors meet with punishment. Religious fraud, deceit under mask of piety, is dealt with very severely. Retribution is not to be escaped. Even J.M. Fuller (S.P.C.K. *Comm. Introd.*), who regards the story as "essentially apocryphal," admits "an edifying element."[84]. This element might perhaps be used with advantage more than it is by missionaries to idolatrous peoples.

> [84] It was told as a story to Miss Yonge when a child by her father (*Life*, 1903, p. 78), and apparently remembered with pleasure through life. So Saml. Johnson: "When I was a boy I have read or heard Bel and the Dragon, Susanna, etc." (*Prayers and Meditations*, Lond. [1905], p. 78).

The sordidness and trickery of heathen priests[85] is contrasted with the uprightness and single-minded devotion of Daniel. His God moreover delivers him, but their gods do not deliver them. The Bel of this history is as dumb as the Baal of I. Kings xviii.; their names and characters quite agree.

> [85] So Butler in his *Hudibras* of the Presbyterian Assembly of Divines:
>
> "Bell (*sic*) and the Dragon's chaplains were
> More moderate than those by far."—(I. III. 1181).

The once flourishing temples of iniquity are conspicuously brought to nought, affording a lesson of confidence and patience to those who fear the Lord. Thus the angry opponents, who made certain of slaying Daniel, were disappointed, and judgment quickly overtook them.

With v. 6 Arnald, *in loc.*, finely contrasts the P.B.V. of Ps. xvi. 2—the God who was estimated by the amount of provisions he consumed, and the God to whom earthly goods were nothing. But the Hebrew will hardly bear the P.B.V. rendering.

The character of Daniel, without fear or reproach, is not out of keeping with that displayed in the canonical book, and in the companion story of Susanna. He affords an example of:

(a) *Courage* in his fearless attacks upon idolatry, attacks which, as the event proved, could not be indulged in with safety. He faces terrible crises at much personal risk, with decision and absence of self-distrust, as in the canonical chapters and in Susanna. He boldly defends his religion when it is called in question, and ousts rival worships.

(b) *Resistance to temptation* in refusing to worship as the king wished. No half compliance is suggested, such as worshipping Bel and God together. Observe how he claims for God to be τὸν ζῶντα Θεόν, while Cyrus only claims for Bel to be ζῶν Θεός (vv. 5, 6, Θ), as noticed under 'Theology.'

(c) *Wisdom*, 'of the serpent,' in his plan for detecting fraud, and in his skill and versatility in choosing suitable means for unveiling each kind of imposture; of which another striking instance occurs in Susanna. He was a man of right understanding, clear insight, and practical sagacity, as shewn by his methods of dealing with opposing forces, moral or physical. As a man of great resource he rapidly adapts himself to fresh conditions.

(d) *Endurance* of persecution for righteousness' sake. One trial overcome, a yet greater presents itself; but with unflinching constancy he faces it and passes unharmed, Ps. lvii. 3, 4.

(e) *Perseverance*, in not resting upon his laurels, won over Bel, but proceeding against the Dragon. His promptitude of resource is not mere rashness, but is combined with steady determination in pursuing his task. As an active and diligent worker he is far-sighted and firm of purpose.

(f) *Gratitude*. On receiving Habakkuk's visit he at once acknowledges God's faithfulness, and addresses himself to the great First Cause immediately (v. 38), as the ever-watchful shaper of events.

(g) *Mindfulness of faith and duty*, by being ever foremost, even in association with a heathen king whose eyes he opens and to whom he acts as a missionary, in shewing hatred of falsehood and love of truth (as in Susanna). Absence of selfishness and willingness to undertake responsibility are manifested.

(h) *Disinterested service* of God in clearing away two great obstacles to his worship. His aims are realised without any trace of self-aggrandisement; for those aims are directed to his Maker's rather than to his own glory.

(i) *Pleasure in God's service*. The tone of the whole story implicitly conveys the idea that Daniel enjoyed, and was happy in the achievement of these works, because they were designed to honour God and to benefit man. Thus he finds his tasks thoroughly interesting and congenial.

It is to be observed that Daniel's character is in contrast with that of everyone in the story, except Habakkuk.

Per contra, Daniel might perhaps be accused of cruelty in his method of slaying the dragon,[86] especially as described in Gaster's Aramaic, and by Josippon ben Gorion, given by Arnald, *in loc.*, from Selden.

[86] J.H. Blunt (*Comm.* on v. 27) makes an unaccountable mistake in supposing that the balls were put into the *statue* of Bel, not eaten by the Dragon. "The composition would not of itself burst the hollow statue either by chymical explosion or mechanical expansion." Almost as ridiculous is the abusive phrase "Offspring of Bel and the Dragon," which Congreve puts into the mouth of Fondlewife in his play of *The Old Bachelor*, Act IV. sc. 4.

In Habakkuk we see *obedience to* a divine command, apparently impossible of execution, for which the way is suddenly made plain. He becomes instrumental in alleviating such a state of affairs as he deplores in i. 4 of his Prophecy: "for the wicked doth compass about the righteous, etc." So in the hymn "Warum betrübst du dich mein Herz?" doubtfully attributed to Hans Sachs, we find the seventh stanza bearing upon this matter:

Des Daniels Gott ihm nicht rergass,
Da er unter den Löwen sass:
Sein Engel sandt er hin,
Und liess ihm Speise bringen gut,
Durch seiner Diener Habakkuk.

Habakkuk's obedience served God's purpose.

In *Cyrus'* character we see something of the impulsiveness of the despotic monarch, giving hasty directions on the spur of the moment as to matters of much importance. But the events of the story exert an educative influence upon his mind, culminating in his sentiments as expressed in v. 41, which apparently imply that Daniel's God was to be his God. Certainly the monarch's testimony proves that his religious opinions had been corrected, and raised above the stage represented in v. 6.

Probably some allegoric, or more strictly 'tropological,' instruction may be drawn from the story. In Bel we are taught to fight against crafty deception however generally believed in; in the Dragon, against fierce, repulsive, and terrifying adversaries. This kind of interpretation is sometimes strained however, as when in Neale's edition of the *Moral Concordances* of St. Antony of Padua (p. 125, n.d.), v. 27 is given as applicable to St. Bartholomew.

An unexpectedly adverse opinion on the use of Bel and the Dragon as a lesson (Nov. 23, matins, old Lectionary) is expressed by J.H. Blunt in his *Directorium Pastorale* (1864, p. 59): "I confess I can see no good which can arise from the public reading to a congregation, composed principally perhaps of young persons, of such lessons as Bel and the Dragon, or Lev. xviii., Deut.

xxii., xxv." Then he adds the following curious note: "It is a fact that a man was once sent into a fit of loud and uncontrollable laughter, although he was honestly preparing for holy orders, by hearing this lesson (Bel and the Dragon) read for the first time in the chapel of a Theological College." One cannot help thinking that this gentleman must have had an abnormally developed sense of humour under exceptionally bad control.

John Wesley exhibits in his Journal (July 5th, 1773) an equally low opinion of the story, though free from ill-timed mirth: "St. Patrick converting 30,000 at one sermon I rank with the History of Bel and the Dragon" (Quoted in *Church Quarterly Review*, Jan. 1902, p. 323).

These opinions seem too contemptuous and inimical to a narrative which yields many valuable lessons. Indeed it may be said of this, as in the Bishops' reply at the Savoy Conference to the Puritan objection to reading the Apocryphal lessons in general: "It is heartily to be wished that sermons were as good" (Procter-Frere, *Hist. of P.B.* 1902, p. 174).

Milton Keynes UK
Ingram Content Group UK Ltd.
UKHW031048120324
439302UK00006B/488

9 789357 944854